Table of Contents

Part Three: Rebuilding Emotional Harmony

Part Four: Love Beyond Fear & Building a New Emotional Legacy

Self-Healing Resources

About the Author

Madhu is a devoted emotional well-being coach, counselor, and psychologist whose life's mission is to help people heal, grow, and transform through the power of love and emotional awareness. With two master's degrees and decades of heartfelt experience ding individuals and families, Madhu has become a beacon of hope for those navigating the stormy waters of emotional pain, self-doubt, and relational challenges.

She believes that *each individual deserves to be emotionally independent*, free from the chains of emotional dependency, manipulation, and suppression. Her gentle yet firm guidance encourages people to break free from control, whether imposed by others or themselves, and discover the joy of living authentically.

Madhu has witnessed how deeply people suffer when they try to control others or bend themselves to fit someone else's expectations. Her work helps people shift from control to connection, from fear to faith, and from pain to purpose. She teaches that healing begins when we choose ourselves, when we honor our feelings, and when we stop living for external validation.

As the President of **First Step Foundation**, Madhu tirelessly works through her NGO to spread awareness about emotional health. Her foundation follows the beautiful motto *"Loka Samasta Sukhino Bhavantu"*- *May all beings be happy and free.* She believes that a healed heart can heal others and that a single act of love can ripple across generations.

Madhu's journey from being a sensitive and shy child to becoming a powerful voice for emotional freedom is woven into her counseling sessions, her community work, and now this book. Through her words, she invites you to take your first step toward healing, to believe in the alchemy of emotions, and to remember that:

"Smile costs nothing, but it enriches your face value."

This book is her heartfelt prayer for you to choose love, embrace your emotions, and live a life full of health, healing, and happiness.

Acknowledgements

As I reflect on the journey of writing this book, my heart overflows with gratitude. This work is not just the result of personal effort, it is the collective energy, love, and support of many souls who have touched my life in countless ways.

To my beloved family-your unwavering love has been my foundation. To my son, the light of my life, your presence has been my strength, my teacher, and my source of infinite joy. You have shown me what unconditional love truly means, and your smile gives me the courage to continue spreading that love to others.

To my dear friends, thank you for standing by me, holding space for my tears, celebrating my small victories, and reminding me of my worth when I forgot. Your loyalty and kindness have carried me through the darkest nights.

To the universe, I bow with reverence. Your divine timing, mysterious synchronicities, and gentle nudges have led me step by step toward my higher purpose. I trust in your plan and am grateful for every challenge, lesson, and breakthrough you've sent my way.

To my mentors, clients, and every soul I've counseled or shared space with, thank you for trusting me with your truth. Your stories, strength, and vulnerability have inspired many of the insights in this book. You've reminded me that we are all mirrors, all students, and all healers.

To the First Step Foundation family, thank you for helping me spread light and love to the world. Together, we carry forward the sacred mission of emotional healing and soulful happiness. May we continue to walk this path guided by our motto: *"Loka Samasta Sukhino Bhavantu"-May all beings be happy and free.*

And finally, **to you, dear reader**, thank you for opening your heart to these pages. Your courage to explore the depth of your emotions is a gift not only to yourself but to the world. My deepest wish is that this book becomes your companion, your mirror, and your reminder that love is not just the answer - it is the key.

This journey is ours to share.
Thank you, from the depths of my soul.

Madhu

Disclaimer

The content of this book, *Emotional Alchemy: Love as the Key to Health, Healing, and Happiness*, is intended solely for informational, inspirational, and educational purposes. It reflects the author's personal journey, professional experience as a counselor and emotional well-being coach, and insights gathered from years of observation, study, and client interactions.

This book does **not** constitute medical, psychiatric, or therapeutic advice. It is **not a substitute** for consultation with a licensed physician, psychologist, psychiatrist, or other qualified healthcare professional. Readers facing emotional, psychological, or physical challenges are strongly encouraged to seek appropriate professional guidance tailored to their individual needs.

The case studies and stories included in this book are **inspired by real-life experiences** but have been **anonymized and modified** to protect the identities of individuals. Names, places, timelines, and other identifying details have been changed, and in many cases, stories are composites created to reflect general themes or emotional patterns. **Any resemblance to actual persons, living or deceased, is purely coincidental.**

The ideas and techniques shared in this book are intended to promote emotional awareness, self-reflection, and healing. However, the effectiveness of any tool or approach will vary by individual. The author and publisher do not guarantee specific outcomes and shall not be held liable for any loss, damage, or injury alleged to have been caused directly or indirectly by the information presented herein.

By reading this book, you acknowledge and accept that your personal use of the information provided is at your discretion and responsibility.

Ultimately, this book is a heartfelt offering to encourage healing, growth, and emotional freedom. The reader is invited to engage with its content with compassion, self-awareness, and an open heart.

This book is for informational purposes only and is not a substitute for professional medical advice."

Introduction

Why Emotions Matter

Emotions are not just fleeting feelings; they are messages from the soul, whispers from the body, and the heartbeat of the human experience. Every emotion you feel, whether it's joy or grief, anger or peace-holds a sacred purpose. Emotions are your inner compass. They help you understand what you need, what needs to be healed, and where love needs to flow.

In a world that often glorifies logic and dismisses feelings, we have forgotten that emotions are our deepest form of intelligence. When we ignore them, suppress them, or mask them to please others, we disconnect from our truest selves. But when we embrace them, when we listen to our tears, honor our heartbreaks, and celebrate our moments of bliss-we unlock the power to transform not just our emotional world, but our physical health and entire life journey.

This book is a return to that wisdom.

The Hidden Language of the Body

Your body speaks what your voice cannot. It stores every unspoken word, every silenced cry, every buried trauma, and every ounce of suppressed love. When emotions are unexpressed or unhealed, the body carries them, sometimes as tension, sometimes as illness, and often as fatigue or chronic discomfort.

Each organ, each body part, is intimately connected to an emotion. The heart weeps when love is withheld. The liver burns with suppressed anger. The stomach churns with anxiety. The back carries the weight of unspoken burdens. And yet, the body is not punishing you-it is simply asking you to listen.

Healing is not about fixing what is broken. It's about remembering what was forgotten, returning to what is whole within you, and releasing what you were never meant to carry.

The Journey of Healing Begins with You

You are the healer you've been searching for.

No one else can walk this path for you, but you are never alone. Through these pages, you will walk hand-in-hand with the wisdom of your emotions, the intelligence of your body, and the infinite power of love. You will meet real stories, simple tools, and profound insights that will help you reconnect with your inner truth and reclaim your well-being.

Emotions are not just fleeting feelings. They are **energy in motion**, and when we learn to direct this energy with awareness and intention, we open the door to a deeply fulfilling life.

This book is more than just insight; it's a guide to transformation. Each chapter offers reflection, stories, and tools to help you recognize your emotional patterns, heal old wounds, and invite more love into your life-starting with the love you give yourself.

So as you turn these pages, I invite you to pause, reflect, and feel. Let this be a journey back to yourself-your true self, the one who knows how to love, heal, and thrive.

Because when you embrace love, you embrace life itself.

This book is not just information; it is a healing space. Let it be your mirror, your map, and your medicine.

No matter what you've been through, no matter how long you've carried pain-healing is possible. Joy is possible. Peace is possible. Love is always possible.

And the journey begins right here with your first breath, your first awareness, and your willingness to say:

"I am ready to feel. I am ready to heal. I am ready to love again."

Welcome home to yourself.

Part One: Understanding Emotions & the Body

Chapter 1:

Emotions - The Invisible Architects of Our Body and Soul

"What you feel is not a weakness. It's the wisdom of your soul trying to speak."

The Unseen Blueprint

Before illness ever appears in the body, it whispers through our emotions.
A quiet ache.
A sense of heaviness.
Tension that won't leave the jaw or neck.
Sleepless nights. Digestive issues. A sudden tightness in the chest.

We often dismiss these signals, treating them as inconveniences or "just stress." But the truth is, our emotions are not side effects. They are **messengers**. They carry the stories we have buried, the pain we haven't voiced, the dreams we've shelved, and the wounds we never dared to look at.

We often talk about emotions as abstract concepts-fleeting feelings that pass through us like clouds. Yet, emotions are anything but intangible. They have a physical presence in our bodies, shaping the way we move, breathe, and even heal. Your body remembers everything, even when your mind tries to forget.

In my years as a healer, I've learned to see emotions as messengers. They speak through tension in our shoulders, aches in our chest, or the churn of an uneasy stomach. Early in my journey, I struggled to connect these physical symptoms with emotional roots, but my experiences with clients and my own life taught me that the body is the canvas on which emotions paint their stories.

My Wake-Up Call

Before becoming a psychologist, I saw emotions as mental experiences separate from the body. That perspective changed during my internship at a counseling department. A patient, Rajesh, arrived with debilitating chest pain. Despite extensive tests, doctors found nothing physically wrong.
When I sat with him, Rajesh revealed the recent loss of his wife. His grief was so overwhelming that his body carried it as physical pain. This encounter

opened my eyes to the profound connection between emotional and physical health.

The Science of Emotions and the Body

Our emotions originate in the brain but are felt throughout the body. Neuroscientists have identified the amygdala, a small almond-shaped structure, as the emotional processing center of the brain. It works with the hypothalamus and the autonomic nervous system to trigger physical responses.

For example:

- **Fear** activates the fight-or-flight response, raising your heart rate and releasing adrenaline.
- **Sadness** slows the body down, often felt as fatigue or heaviness in the chest.
- **Joy** releases endorphins, creating a lightness or warmth that feels almost tangible.

Understanding this connection is crucial because unresolved emotions can linger in the body, manifesting as chronic pain, illness, or fatigue. Each emotion has a physical home. Anxiety lives in the gut. Grief sits in the chest. Resentment clenches the shoulders. Fear tightens the throat. Unworthiness seeps into the spine. These emotional energies, when left unacknowledged, don't just disappear; rather, they **embed themselves** into the tissues, muscles, and cells.

Scientific studies now confirm what ancient healing traditions have always known: emotions directly influence immune function, hormone balance, blood flow, and even how genes express themselves.

But this is not a book of fear- it's a book of **hope**.
 Because just as emotions can wound, they can also **heal**.

When we learn to listen, honor, and gently release what we've carried, our bodies respond with vitality. Our hearts soften. Our breath returns. Our cells awaken.

My Story: From Silence to Soul

As a child, I was gentle, shy, and deeply sensitive. I felt everything.
 I cried easily, feared conflict, and often struggled to understand the intense emotions within me. Society taught me to be "strong" by hiding pain, smiling through heartbreak, and pretending everything was fine.

But it wasn't fine.

It was in the silence that I first felt the ache of emotional suppression. And later, in college, love broke me open. A heartbreak that shattered me also revealed a hidden truth: **emotions are not the enemy - they are the key to everything.**

I began listening, first to myself, then to others. I saw patterns between unspoken grief and physical illness, between unresolved anger and chronic fatigue. I watched people transform, not by denying their emotions, but by **meeting them** with love and curiosity.

And that became my life's work: helping others understand that healing is not just about medicine or therapy- it's about coming home to yourself.

The Power of Awareness
Emotions are not problems to solve; they are signals to heed. Just as physical pain warns us of injury, emotional discomfort urges us to pay attention to areas of our lives that need care and change.

What This Book Offers You

This book is an emotional map, one that walks you through your body and helps you decode what your symptoms might be trying to say. Each chapter explores an organ or area of the body, uncovering the emotional roots often hidden beneath physical pain.

You'll read stories, my experiences with people and their stories, and those of people who dared to feel, to heal, and to live again.
 You'll learn practical tools, insights, and gentle practices to support your own journey.

And most importantly, you'll be reminded that you are not broken, you are becoming whole.

Emotions Are the Bridge, Not the Barrier

We live in a world that often rushes us out of our feelings.
"Move on."
"Be strong."
"Let it go."

But emotions are not detours. They are the way through.
 They are the bridge between trauma and transformation, between surviving and truly living.
 The question is not, "Why am I feeling this?"
 The question is, "What is this feeling here to teach me?"

Practical Steps for Readers

1.   **Body Scanning**: Spend five minutes daily scanning your body for tension or discomfort. Notice where emotions might be residing.
2.   **Name Your Emotion**: When you feel an ache or tension, ask yourself what emotion it might represent. Is it fear? Sadness? Anger?
3.   **Move Your Body**: Emotions can get "stuck" in the body. Gentle stretches or yoga can help release pent-up feelings.
4.   **Express Yourself**: Journaling, talking to a trusted friend, or seeking therapy can help process and release emotions.

My Commitment to You

This book is a blend of science, stories, and strategies. It's an invitation to understand your emotions and their impact on your body. As you read, you'll meet people who courageously faced their emotional truths and learn how their transformations inspired my journey.

Final Thoughts: The Beginning of Coming Home

You don't have to fix everything today.
 You don't need to "get rid" of your emotions.
 You simply need to start listening.

This book will walk beside you, chapter by chapter, emotion by emotion, breath by breath. It's not a quick fix, it's a **return to yourself**. A remembering of your inner power, your right to feel, and your ability to heal through love, awareness, and truth.

In the next chapter, we'll begin our journey with the **heart,** the emotional epicenter of love, loss, longing, and courage. The heart is not just a pump; it is the keeper of your deepest truths.

Let's begin the healing together!

Chapter 2:

What matters most - Love or heart?

The Heart: Not Just an Organ, but an Oracle

When we think of the heart, we often reduce it to a biological pump, an organ working tirelessly to circulate blood. But those of us who have truly *felt*: who have loved, lost, longed, or broken, know the heart is far more than muscle and chambers. It is the seat of our deepest emotions. A sacred space where joy blooms, grief echoes, and love leaves its mark.

The heart does not simply react to emotion but holds them. It remembers. And when that emotional weight becomes too heavy to bear, the heart lets us know. Not with words, but through sensation: a racing beat, a tightening in the chest, a dull ache, a piercing pain. Science may call it psychosomatic; the soul calls it truth.

We've all heard the term "heartbreak," but how many of us truly understand that it's not just a metaphor? The body feels it. And for some, it becomes a defining moment, a gateway to awareness, or a collapse into silence.

My Own Brush with Heartache

Heartbreak isn't always romantic. Sometimes, it arrives through quiet cracks in our purpose-moments where love is met with loss, where presence is not enough to save a soul. One such moment carved itself into the earliest years of my professional life, and it never truly left.

His name was Aryan. A gentle soul with tired eyes and a soft voice. He was only in his early twenties but carried the exhaustion of someone far older. Beneath his silence was a well of pain-childhood trauma, abandonment, rejection. He came to the help centre with the hope of healing, and I offered him my heart, my time, and my full presence.

Week by week, I saw flickers of light-moments of laughter, trust, glimpses of hope. I believed in his healing more than he believed in himself. But then, one day, he stopped showing up, and his dysfunctional family stopped him. No messages. No calls. Just silence.

A few weeks later, I received the news that Aryan had taken his own life.

The world stopped.

No textbook, no lecture, no supervision had ever prepared me for this kind of ache. It wasn't just professional grief, it was *personal*. It broke something open inside me. My chest felt hollow and heavy at the same time, as if my own heart had absorbed his unspoken pain.

That moment changed how I understood the heart not as a concept, but as a living, feeling being within us. Since Aryan, I have never looked at emotional suffering the same way. I approach each person with reverence, knowing how quietly pain can sit behind a smile, and how sacred it is when someone chooses to share it.

That experience changed me. It taught me that emotional pain is not just something we *think*, but it's something we *carry*. My heart ached, not metaphorically, but quite literally. Aryan's story became a permanent part of my journey. It taught me to approach every client with deeper presence, compassion, and awareness of the unspoken.

His memory reminds me daily of the silent battles people fight, the urgency of connection, and the sacred responsibility we hold when someone trusts us with their pain. Since then, I've worked not only to support healing in others but also to raise awareness about the invisible weight of emotional suffering and the power of love, presence, and understanding in lifting it.

The Heart-Brain Connection

The heart and brain are in constant communication, sending signals through the autonomic nervous system. Here's how different emotions influence the heart:

- Joy and Love: Activate the parasympathetic system, slowing the heart rate and creating a sense of calm.
- Fear and Anger: Trigger the sympathetic system, speeding up the heart and preparing the body for action.
- Grief and Sadness: Can cause a sensation of heaviness or tightness in the chest, sometimes called "broken heart syndrome" (Takotsubo cardiomyopathy).

Studies have shown that people with unresolved emotional distress are at higher risk of cardiovascular issues, highlighting the importance of emotional health for heart health.

Ria's Journey Through Heartbreak

Ria's Story - When Love Becomes a Lesson

Ria, a bright and driven 28-year-old entrepreneur, walked into my office after a soul-crushing breakup. Her eyes were dull, her shoulders slumped forward, and her first words were barely a whisper:
"It feels like my chest is caving in."

She wasn't exaggerating. Her body mirrored her emotional collapse. She suffered from heart palpitations, sleepless nights, and sudden waves of panic that left her breathless and trembling. Despite multiple visits to doctors and clear medical reports, the pain in her chest never eased. That's because the ache wasn't physical; it was emotional. Her heart was bruised, bleeding from a wound no scan could ever detect.

As we slowly unraveled her story, a deeper truth emerged.

Ria had loved Ram for eleven long years with her whole heart unconditionally.

In those eleven years, she celebrated his smallest victories, stood by him during his worst failures, and loved him when he couldn't even be kind to her. But while she gave him her days, her dreams, and her devotion, he gave her only what was convenient. A few texts, occasional meetups when he was free, and promises that never turned into actions.

What hurt Ria the most wasn't just his neglect, but the way he flirted openly with other women, even in front of her. Every time she brought it up, he laughed it off, accused her of being "too emotional," or simply vanished until she apologized for reacting.

Despite all this, Ria held on. She was a believer. She believed in the Universe, in karma, and most of all, in true love.

"If I love him truly, he'll love me the same someday," she often said, her voice a fragile mix of hope and heartbreak.

But days turned into years. And years turned into an exhausting emotional cycle of giving and hoping, while never receiving.

What Ria didn't realize was that in loving Ram unconditionally, she had forgotten to love herself at all.

Her boundaries had blurred. She overgave. She overextended. She forgave when she should have walked away. Slowly but surely, she became emotionally bankrupt. Her world had narrowed to Ram's moods, Ram's needs, Ram's timings, and in the process, she had stopped hearing the voice of her own soul.

It took months of deep emotional work, guided self-reflection, and compassionate inner healing before she finally said what I had been waiting to hear:

"I thought love meant never giving up on someone. But now I know, real love should never ask you to give up on yourself."

Ria cried that day not out of pain, but relief. She finally allowed herself to grieve, not just the loss of Ram, but the loss of the girl who had once begged for scraps of love. And in doing so, she began a new chapter.

She started loving herself the way she once loved him-with passion, patience, and presence. She learned to say no without guilt. She learned to rest without shame. She danced again, dreamed again, and slept peacefully without waiting for a message that never came.

Ria's journey wasn't about forgetting Ram. It was about remembering Ria.

And the most beautiful part? Today, she is still a giver, but now, she gives from a place of wholeness, not desperation. Her love is no longer a plea- it's a gift. First to herself, and then to the world.

When a woman reclaims her heart, heartbreak cannot even defeat her.

When Ria came to us, together, we worked on:

- **Heart-Centered Breathing**: Inhaling deeply with hands over the heart, visualizing each breath as golden light, filling the chest with warmth and compassion.
- **Gratitude Practices**: Shifting focus from what was lost to what remained, her strength, her support system, her own evolving self.
- **Reframing Love**: Love was no longer something to *get* from others; it became something she *cultivated* within.

Practical Steps for Readers

If you've ever felt emotional pain in your chest, these practices can help:

Heart-Centered Breathing: Place your hand over your heart and take slow, deep breaths. Focus on sending warmth to your chest.

Name Your Emotions: When your heart feels heavy, try naming the emotions you're experiencing. This can help you process them.

Embrace Movement: Gentle exercises like walking or yoga can help release pent-up emotions in the chest.

Connect with Others: Sharing your feelings with a trusted friend or therapist can provide relief and perspective.

Final Reflections: What Matters Most?

So, what matters more-love or the heart?

The truth is, they are not separate.

The heart *is* the house of love. And love is the language the heart understands. When we choose to live from love, not just romantic love, but compassion, empathy, and presence, we protect the heart. We strengthen it. We allow it to grow even through grief.

My journey, Aryan's memory, and Ria's transformation all point to this truth: the heart may break, but it does not give up. It heals. It remembers. And in its brokenness, it often becomes more open, more wise, more ready to love again.

In the next chapter, we will journey into the gut-often called the second brain, where instincts, fear, and inner knowing dwell. There, you'll learn how to listen to the quiet whispers of intuition and reclaim the wisdom that has always lived inside you.

Chapter 3:

The Gut - The Silent Guardian of Fear and Intuition

The Gut: Our Emotional Compass

Our gut does much more than digest food. It feels, senses, and responds to the world around us. Often referred to as our "second brain," the gut contains over 100 million neurons within the enteric nervous system. That's why we feel butterflies in our stomach before a big moment or experience a sinking feeling when something just doesn't feel right.

We often talk about "gut feelings" as passing instincts, fleeting sensations we notice and then brush aside. But what if I told you your gut is not just reacting, but it's remembering? Feeling. Knowing. Speaking. It is your body's silent guardian, the compass that senses danger before it arrives, unease before a word is spoken, and truth even before the mind can process it.

The gut is not merely the site of digestion. It is the home of a second intelligence - your **emotional compass**. With over 100 million neurons in its own nervous system (the *enteric nervous system*), your gut is in constant dialogue with your brain, your heart, and your emotions

In my practice, I've come to see the gut as a wise and intuitive emotional compass. It speaks to us through discomfort, tension, and even silence. It often knows the truth before the mind catches up. Many of my clients have discovered deep emotional healing simply by learning to listen to their gut and trust what it is trying to say.

The Moment I Ignored My Own Compass

I was younger, eager, and perhaps a little too willing to silence my instincts for the sake of "opportunity." A prestigious organization offered me a leading role in a high-profile emotional wellness project. The words sounded beautiful. The contract looked generous. My peers congratulated me.

But my stomach churned.

Every time I thought of saying yes, I felt a dull, unshakable discomfort in my core. It wasn't fear of failure, it was something else. Something quieter. A whisper of *mismatch*, a dissonance I couldn't quite name.

I said yes anyway.

Within weeks, I was drowning-not in work, but in emotional exhaustion. My gut wasn't reacting to the workload. It was reacting to misalignment. I was working with people who spoke about empathy but lacked it, promoting healing while operating in an environment that felt emotionally sterile and competitive.

My health began to suffer. My digestion faltered, my energy crashed, and I started dreading each morning.

Eventually, I stepped away. It wasn't failure - it was freedom. That chapter taught me something I now teach every client: **If your gut says no, it's not fear. It's guidance.** The body always knows. We just have to stop overriding it.

The Science of the Gut-Brain Axis

The gut and brain communicate through the vagus nerve, a two-way communication superhighway. When you experience fear or anxiety, your brain sends signals to the gut, triggering physical symptoms like:

- Nausea
- Stomach cramps
- Bloating
- Diarrhea or constipation

This is not "in your head"-this is your head and gut working together. In fact, 90% of serotonin (the happiness hormone) is produced in the gut. That means your emotional balance quite literally begins in your belly. This gut-brain connection is why conditions like Irritable Bowel Syndrome (IBS) are often linked to stress and anxiety. Conversely, an unhealthy gut can send distress signals to the brain, amplifying emotional issues.

Meera's Rise from Within

Meera, a 35-year-old mother of twins and a small business owner, met me not because she was anxious-but because her gut was constantly in distress.

"I feel bloated, uncomfortable, and exhausted every single day," she said. "But the doctors keep saying nothing is wrong."

Nothing was "wrong" physically, but Meera was emotionally dehydrated. She carried the weight of caring for her children, managing her business, and suppressing her own needs. Her body became the messenger her words refused to speak.

We didn't start with diet plans or medication.

We began with **awareness**.

Meera was guided to slow down and track the connection between her emotions and her symptoms. She discovered that every time she said *yes* when she meant *no*, her gut flared up. When she felt disrespected but remained silent, her digestion revolted. Her gut had become her voice.

Through breathwork, self-honoring practices, and journaling, Meera began to shift. She started asserting her needs-not aggressively, but clearly. She simplified her work hours. She allowed herself moments of joy without guilt. Over time, Mira's symptoms improved. She felt more in control of her life and began to trust her gut as a guide, not an enemy.

Months later, her symptoms diminished.

Her gut didn't just heal, it **guided** her home to herself.

Listening to Your Gut

Your gut never lies. It's a wise part of you, whispering truths you may not yet be ready to hear. Tuning in to its signals can guide you toward better decisions, deeper healing, and greater peace.

Your Gut as Your Inner Guardian: How to Begin Listening

Start noticing. Your gut is speaking in subtle tones. It does not scream, it *whispers*. These gentle practices can help you tune in:

- **The Belly Check-In**

Place one hand on your heart, the other on your belly. Ask yourself: *What do I truly feel right now?* Wait. Let the answer rise. Don't analyze. Just notice.

- **Decision by Sensation**

Before a big choice, sit quietly and visualize each option. Notice how your stomach responds. Does it expand or contract? Feel open or heavy? The gut responds faster than the mind-trust that.

- **Cleanse the Clutter**

Support your gut physically by reducing processed foods, incorporating probiotics, and drinking warm, calming teas like chamomile or fennel. A peaceful gut creates emotional clarity.

- **Voice the Unspeakable**

Your gut often holds what you haven't voiced. Start writing or speaking your truth aloud in safe spaces. Unspoken fear is stored in the body. Expressed fear begins to dissolve.

Final Thoughts

The gut is more than an organ. It is a storyteller, revealing the unspoken truths that live within us. It holds our fears, our instincts, and our unexpressed emotions. Through Mira's healing and my own missteps, I learned that when we ignore our gut, we silence a part of our deepest wisdom.

Listening to it doesn't mean life becomes easier, but it does become clearer. And clarity, when paired with courage, is where transformation and emotional healing begin.

In the Next Chapter...

We'll breathe.

In Chapter 4, we journey into the **lungs** - the breath of life, the rhythm of release. Through stories of grief and grounding, you'll discover how breath connects you to the present moment and how each inhale and exhale becomes an invitation to let go, renew, and return to wholeness.

Chapter 4:

The Lungs and Breath -When the Lungs Learn to Let Go

"The breath is the bridge which connects life to consciousness." - Thích Nhất Hạnh

The Breath of Life

Breathing is the very essence of life. From the moment we are born, our lungs expand with that first miraculous inhale, connecting us to the world. Yet, most of us move through our days unaware of this quiet, constant rhythm that keeps us alive. Our breath reflects our inner world. When we are at peace, the breath flows freely.. Our lungs, like our hearts, feel everything. Our lungs don't just move air, they move emotion. They hold grief, longing, unsaid words, and the ache of separation. When we're wounded emotionally, the breath shortens. When we feel safe, it flows like a stream. In truth, the lungs don't just support life - they reflect how deeply we are willing to live.

In my work and life, I've seen how love, acceptance, and compassion have the power to restore not only our spirit but also our breath. Love isn't just a soft feeling; it is a medicine. When we allow love to soften our pain and open our hearts, our lungs respond with ease. We can breathe again.

Breath as a Mirror of Emotion

In Chinese medicine and many ancient healing traditions, the lungs are considered the seat of grief. Modern science now supports this wisdom: chronic stress and unresolved sorrow can suppress immune response, reduce lung capacity, and even increase vulnerability to respiratory illness.
But there is another side to this truth; healing our emotional lives can also restore our breath.
When we learn to let go, not to forget or suppress, but to soften, we create space. And in that space, breath returns, like a long-lost friend.
Emotional landscape of the Lungs

Our lungs and our emotions are closely linked. When we hold onto grief, anger, or disappointment, we unconsciously trap that energy in the chest. The lungs, tender and sensitive, often carry the weight of unexpressed sorrow.
Scientifically, the connection between breath and emotion is deeply rooted. The lungs and heart are regulated by our nervous system. When we feel sadness or tension, the sympathetic nervous system is activated, leading to shallow, quick breathing. Over time, this can exhaust the lungs, creating fatigue and vulnerability to disease. But when we shift toward love, presence, and compassion, the parasympathetic system takes over. Our breathing deepens. Healing begins.

Client Story: Aarav and His Daughter's Love

Aarav was 50 when he came to me, recovering from a severe bout of pneumonia that had left him with lingering breathing difficulties. Once an active and energetic father, he now avoided physical activity and struggled with feelings of helplessness.

"I feel like my lungs are failing me," he said. "I can't even play with my daughter without gasping for air."

Aarav also carried the emotional weight of his wife, who had passed away two years earlier, and he hadn't fully grieved her loss. His lungs, once strong and vital, seemed to mirror his grief, constricted and weak.

During our sessions, Aarav opened up about his struggles as a single parent and his fear of not being enough for his 8-year-old daughter, Meera. "She's my world," he said, tears streaming down his face. "But I don't know how to show her the love she deserves when I feel so broken."

We began working on healing his lungs through both physical and emotional practices:

1.   **Breathwork**: Aarav practiced slow, deep breathing exercises to strengthen his lungs and calm his nervous system.
2.   **Grief Release**: Together, we explored his unspoken grief for his wife. Through journaling and guided visualizations, Aarav found ways to honor her memory without being consumed by pain.
3.   **Connection with Meera**: I encouraged Aarav to share his emotions with Meera, not as a burden but as a way of deepening their bond.

One day, Aarav brought Meera to a session. She held a crumpled drawing in her hand that was a picture of a big red heart with tiny lungs inside it. "Daddy, I drew this for you," she said. "Your lungs are in my heart, so they'll always get better."

That moment was transformative. Aarav realized that love wasn't about being perfect; it was about showing up, being present, and letting himself be vulnerable.

With Meera's encouragement, Aarav started walking with her every evening. At first, he could only manage a short distance, but with time and her gentle support, his stamina improved. More importantly, he rediscovered joy.

Months later, Aarav shared a moment that brought tears to my eyes. "We were flying kites at the park," he said, smiling. "I was running with Meera, and for the first time in years, I felt like I could breathe-really breathe. She healed me."

Real Story: A Decade of Lung Disease and a Journey to Acceptance

There's another story, close to my heart. I've known someone for many years who was diagnosed with a chronic lung disease more than a decade ago. Despite treatments and care, his condition kept worsening. When I spent time with him, I began to observe his emotional patterns and how they mirrored his physical suffering.

He struggled to accept life as it was. He tried to control situations, people, and outcomes according to his rigid perceptions. If his family or loved ones didn't align with his expectations, he would become frustrated, angry, and deeply stressed. He carried resentment like a weight in his chest, and each unmet expectation tightened his lungs a little more.

Over time, his health deteriorated. Doctors couldn't fully explain why his condition persisted despite medication. But then, something shifted.
He began exploring trauma healing. Slowly, he started to recognize that his suffering wasn't coming from outside circumstances, but it was coming from within. His lungs weren't failing because of the world, but because he was not allowing life to simply be as it is.

He began to soften.

He started to let go of the need to control. He began practicing acceptance and letting things unfold, without force or resistance. He made space for the wishes and feelings of his children, his wife, and others, learning to support them instead of directing them. His anger melted into compassion. His rigid thinking turned into understanding. And with every small act of love and surrender, his breath grew deeper.

Now, he is relaxed. Free. He accepts life moment by moment, without resistance. He no longer battles his circumstances, but he flows with them. And his lungs, once burdened by emotional armor, are finally breathing with joy. His healing came not from medicine alone, but from a transformation of the heart.

The Healing Power of Love

Love, when lived, and not just felt, can heal. It restores not just relationships but also the body. The lungs, which carry the rhythm of life, respond beautifully to emotions like forgiveness, acceptance, and compassion.

Love isn't just an abstract concept; it's a tangible force that expands our capacity to breathe and thrive. Aarav's story shows that love, whether for a partner, a child, or even oneself, can bring life back to our lungs.

Here are gentle ways to nurture your lungs through emotional healing:

- Practice Deep Breathing: Breathe in slowly through the nose, hold for a few seconds, then exhale gently. Let each breath be an act of kindness toward yourself.
- Accept What Is: Let go of the need to fix or control. Trust that life is unfolding exactly as it needs to.
- Express Your Emotions: Write, speak, or cry when needed. Releasing sadness makes room for love. If there are words you've held in grief, gratitude, or goodbye, give them voice. Even whispering them in solitude can bring relief.
- Prioritize Connection: Be present with your loved ones. Small moments of tenderness carry immense healing.
- Compassionate Breathing: Practice 4-4-6 breathing - inhale for 4 seconds, hold for 4, and exhale for 6. Let each exhale be a gentle release of what no longer serves you.

- Lead with Compassion: Replace judgment with understanding. See yourself and others through the lens of love.
- Let Nature Breathe With You: Spend time outdoors. Trees breathe, too. Let your lungs remember what freedom feels like.

Final Thoughts

The lungs are a bridge between the physical and emotional, connecting us to life and to one another. The lungs are not just organs of breath, but they are vessels of emotion. They store our sorrows, hold our unspoken words, and respond to how deeply we allow ourselves to live. Aarav's journey, and the story of a man who chose healing over control, remind us that we always have a choice: to contract with fear or to expand with love. Our lungs respond to all of this. They are not just organs; they are messengers.

Your lungs are sacred. They are not just a part of your body, they are part of your story. When you choose to let go of emotional burdens, when you allow yourself to accept, forgive, and flow, your lungs respond. They open. They heal. They breathe.

Let this chapter be your gentle reminder. You don't have to carry the weight of the world. You deserve to breathe deeply, freely, and joyfully.

In every inhale, there is hope. In every exhale, a letting go.

Let your breath be your teacher. Let love be your medicine.

In the next chapter, we'll explore the shoulders which are often the silent carriers of our burdens. Through stories of release and renewal, we'll discover how to free ourselves from the invisible loads we carry and move through life with lightness and strength.

Chapter 5:

The Silent Weight - Shoulders and the Burden We Carry

The Shoulders: Our Unspoken Load

Our shoulders carry more than muscle and bone, they carry our stories, our struggles, our responsibilities. They hold the silent weight of everything we didn't say, couldn't let go of, or felt too responsible to release.

Have you ever noticed how your shoulders rise and tense when you're under pressure or emotionally overwhelmed? That's not just stress - it's your body protecting itself from what the heart hasn't processed. The shoulders are often the first to respond and the last to relax.

For many people, chronic shoulder tension is not just a physical issue but a sign of emotional overload. It's where we "brace ourselves" against life-holding tension from unhealed trauma, fear of failure, or feeling like we must hold everything together.

When Shoulders Become Armor

In my work, I've observed how the shoulders can become emotional armor. Many of us walk through life weighed down, not by external circumstances, but by internalized pressure: to be strong, to succeed, to not disappoint.

One client, **Priya**, a 39-year-old single mother and small business owner, met me with persistent shoulder pain that no therapy or medication seemed to touch. She had become the emotional pillar for her children, her aging parents, and her team at work. Her shoulders were tight, almost frozen, as though they were clenching onto her sense of duty.

As we explored her emotional landscape, she shared, "I can't afford to fall apart. If I collapse, everything around me will too."

But in trying to hold up the world, Priya was losing herself. Her body had become a battleground between resilience and exhaustion.

We worked on unlearning this internalized pressure. Through somatic exercises, emotional release techniques, and gentle affirmations like "I am allowed to rest," Priya slowly began letting go of the burden. As she learned to delegate, say no, and honor her needs, her pain began to soften. Her shoulders finally dropped not in defeat, but in freedom.

The Shoulders and Suppressed Emotions

Emotionally, the shoulders often store:

- **Guilt** - for not doing or being "enough"
- **Shame** - for past actions or perceived failures
- **Fear** - of being seen as weak or vulnerable
- **Over-responsibility** - carrying others' pain or problems as your own

All of these emotions, when left unexpressed, tighten the shoulders like a noose. This chronic tension can lead to headaches, neck stiffness, and even numbness in the arms, a sign that the body is calling for emotional release.

Real Story: The Warrior Who Finally Laid Down His Sword

I once worked with a man named **Major Arvind**, a retired army officer who appeared physically fit but was emotionally rigid. After years of discipline and sacrifice, his posture was impeccable: shoulders pulled back, chest out, always ready to act. But his smile was strained, and his body was in constant pain.

In one of our sessions, I asked him gently, "What are you still fighting?"

He broke down in tears. He had never grieved the loss of fellow soldiers. He had never cried for the family moments he missed. He had been everyone's strength for so long that he forgot how to be soft.

We practiced guided shoulder release meditations, grief rituals, and storytelling sessions where he could finally speak about the war-not just the one on the battlefield, but the one inside him. As his emotions flowed, so did his physical pain. For the first time in decades, he allowed his shoulders to soften and his heart to open.

Healing Practices for the Shoulders

If your shoulders feel heavy, tight, or in pain, here are gentle practices to explore:

1. Emotional Scanning

Take a few minutes daily to close your eyes and ask, "What am I carrying today that isn't mine to hold?" Breathe and release.

2. Movement Therapy

Engage in gentle shoulder rolls, yoga stretches like eagle arms, or intuitive dance. Movement allows stuck emotions to flow.

3. Forgiveness Work

Often, the heaviest burden is the anger or guilt we hold. Write letters (you don't have to send them) to forgive others, or yourself.

4. Say "No" Without Guilt

Reclaim your space by setting boundaries. Saying "no" is a powerful way to say "yes" to your well-being.

5. Ask for Help

Being strong doesn't mean carrying everything alone. Allowing yourself to lean on others is also a strength.

Final Thoughts: Shoulders Are for Holding, Not Hiding

Your shoulders were never meant to carry the world. They were meant to dance, to stretch, to hug, to embrace. They're not meant to be a prison of pain, but a bridge of strength and tenderness.

When you choose to release the burdens you've carried for too long, you don't become weak - you become real. You become free.

Your body remembers what your heart tries to forget. And when the shoulders finally let go, you'll feel it-not just in your muscles, but in your soul.

Chapter 6:

The Back and Suppressed Anger

The Back: Carrying the Weight of the World

Our back is both our strength and our burden. It holds us upright, supports our daily movements, and bears the load of life's physical and emotional demands. Yet, when anger and unresolved responsibilities build up, the back often becomes a canvas for this tension and manifests as stiffness, pain, or even chronic conditions.

Anger is a natural, necessary emotion, but when we push it down, pretend it doesn't exist, or fear expressing it, it doesn't disappear. It buries itself deep within us and tightening muscles, stiffening joints, and creating discomfort that no physical treatment can fully cure. Emotional burdens, especially those rooted in guilt, obligation, and resentment, often express themselves in the back.

Similarly, unacknowledged responsibilities, whether personal or professional, can accumulate like invisible bricks, making it harder to stand tall.

A Poem: The Weight I Bear

I carry the weight you do not see,
Responsibilities piled upon me.
Each unspoken word, each silent cry,
Lodged in my spine as time drifts by.

Anger unvoiced, it burns inside,
A fire unlit, where shadows reside.
But love and strength can ease this strain,
Freeing my back from its silent pain.

The Burden of Suppressed Anger

Anger is often misunderstood. It is not something to be feared or judged, and it is a messenger. It tells us when our boundaries have been crossed, when something isn't right. But if we don't listen, that anger begins to speak through the body.

- **Upper back pain** is often connected to emotional burdens such as guilt or the pressure to take care of others.
- **Mid-back tension** tends to reflect unresolved anger and frustration we haven't been able to express.
- **Lower back pain** can be tied to financial insecurity, feelings of instability, or taking on responsibilities beyond our limits.

Healing begins when we stop ignoring the emotional roots of our pain.

In my practice, I've learned that acknowledging anger, rather than denying it, is the first step toward healing.

Client Story: Raj's Fight with Invisible Burdens

Raj, a 42-year-old software engineer, came to me with persistent back pain that no amount of medication or therapy could resolve. In his words, "It feels like I'm carrying the weight of the world on my shoulders."

As we explored his life story, Raj opened up about the emotional load he had been carrying for years. He was the sole provider for not just his immediate family, but also his parents and siblings. He had been giving endlessly-financially, emotionally, and mentally, without ever expressing how exhausted he felt.

"I don't want to complain," he said, "but sometimes I feel like I'm disappearing under the pressure."

Raj had never allowed himself to feel angry. He believed that being a good son, brother, and husband meant self-sacrifice. But that belief was breaking his back literally.

Through sessions, Raj slowly began to heal:

- **He acknowledged his anger** through unsent letters to his family. Putting feelings into words gave his pain a voice.
- **He practiced mindful movement** like yoga and gentle stretching, becoming aware of where emotion lived in his body.
- **He set boundaries** by beginning to say no in small ways without guilt or explanation.
- **He asked for support** and communicated clearly. During a family meeting, he gently said, "I need you to contribute. I can't do this alone anymore."

To his surprise, his siblings responded with understanding. Over the following weeks, Raj's pain started to ease. But the deeper change was emotional. He felt lighter, more in control, and most importantly, free.

"For the first time in years," he shared, "I feel like I can stand tall not just physically, but emotionally too."

Are you Carrying Emotional Weight?

If you're experiencing back pain or tension, consider whether suppressed anger or unresolved responsibilities might be contributing. Here are some signs to watch for:

- Persistent pain that isn't relieved by physical treatments.
- Feeling "trapped" or "weighed down" in your daily life.
- Resentment or frustration that you struggle to express.
- Fatigue, even after rest.

Ask yourself:

- Am I holding back anger because I fear confrontation?
- Am I carrying responsibilities that should be shared?
- Do I feel appreciated for all that I give?
- Is there a part of me that just wants to be heard?

The pain in your back may be more than physical. It may be an emotional weight you were never meant to carry alone.

Lightening the Load

Releasing suppressed anger and hidden responsibility requires patience, compassion, and courage. Begin by inviting awareness into your daily life.

- **Move mindfully.** Practices like yoga, tai chi, or simple daily stretching help you reconnect with your body and release built-up tension.
- **Express what you feel.** Journaling, art, and open conversations can give anger and frustration a safe outlet.
- **Ask for help.** Sharing your responsibilities doesn't make you weak; rather, it makes you wise. Let others support you.
- **Set healthy boundaries.** You are not obligated to overextend yourself. Saying "no" can be an act of self-love.
- **Offer yourself compassion.** You are doing your best. You deserve kindness from others and from yourself.

Final Thoughts

The back is our pillar of strength, but even pillars need care and support. You were not meant to carry everything alone. When we suppress anger, we carry it in our bodies. But when we allow ourselves to feel, to express, and to release, we create space for healing.

Like Raj, you too can stand tall again, strong, clear, and emotionally free.

In the next chapter, we will explore how **gratitude**, carried in open hands and an open heart, has the power to heal not just the mind, but the body and soul. Through the practice of gratitude, you will discover how to transform pain into presence, burden into blessing, and survival into true, soulful living.

Let's take that next step together with open hands and grateful hearts.

Chapter 7:

The Healing Power of Gratitude

Gratitude: The Touch of Healing in Our Hands

In the previous chapter, we explored the back and our foundation of strength and burden. We saw how suppressed anger and unspoken responsibilities can weigh us down, both physically and emotionally. Now, we move forward to a more open, expansive energy: the hands - our sacred tools of giving and receiving. And what better offering can we place in our hands than gratitude?

Gratitude is often spoken of as a virtue, a polite gesture, or a fleeting feeling when life is kind. But in truth, **gratitude is medicine,** a healing balm not just for the soul but also for the body. When we consciously open our hands to appreciate life, even in the smallest of ways, we invite transformation into our nervous system, our immune health, and even the rhythm of our hearts.

Through my journey as an emotional well-being coach, I've seen one common thread among those who begin to truly heal: **they find something to be grateful for, even amid their pain**. That simple shift opens the heart, calms the mind, and speaks gently to the body, whispering: *It's okay to feel better now.*

Gratitude and the Body

The science behind gratitude is impressive. Research shows that practicing gratitude can reduce stress, lower blood pressure, and improve sleep. It strengthens the immune system and promotes a heart-healthy environment by reducing inflammation. Gratitude activates regions in the brain responsible for regulating emotions, increasing motivation, and decreasing stress. It reduces cortisol, the hormone associated with chronic stress and inflammation, and boosts the production of dopamine and serotonin-neurotransmitters linked to happiness and well-being.

But perhaps one of the most powerful aspects of gratitude is its ability to shift our perspective. It helps us focus on the positive, reducing the mental and physical effects of stress and anxiety. When we express gratitude, our minds become calmer, our bodies more relaxed, and our immune systems more resilient.

When we choose to practice gratitude regularly, even for just a few minutes a day, we experience powerful health benefits:

- Lower blood pressure and heart rate

- Improved sleep quality and longer restful periods

- A stronger immune response

- Reduced symptoms of anxiety and depression

Gratitude, in essence, brings the body back to a place of balance, harmony, and trust.

The Shift of Perspective: From What's Missing to What's Present

Gratitude is not the denial of pain. It's not pretending everything is perfect. It's the courageous choice to look beyond the struggle and see what is still beautiful, still kind, still worth holding onto.

When we're stuck in emotional pain, whether it's anger in the back, grief in the chest, or fear in the gut, our bodies contract, brace, and close. But gratitude opens us up. It softens our rigidity and creates space for healing.

This is the moment when the hands come into play: they are no longer clenched in frustration or held tightly in fear. They open gently in appreciation, ready to receive the present moment with grace.

The Connection between Gratitude and Health

1. **Stress Reduction**: Chronic stress is a silent killer, leading to high blood pressure, weakened immune function, and poor mental health. Gratitude has the ability to reduce the body's production of stress hormones, particularly cortisol, allowing the body to heal and regenerate.

2.   **Heart Health**: Grateful people tend to have lower levels of heart disease. One study found that people who practiced gratitude had a 23% lower risk of developing heart disease. This is likely because gratitude reduces the stress and anxiety that contribute to high blood pressure and inflammation.
3.   **Improved Sleep**: Gratitude improves sleep quality. People who keep a gratitude journal or consciously reflect on positive experiences before bed report falling asleep faster, staying asleep longer, and feeling more rested.
4.   **Stronger Immunity**: Regular practice of gratitude can increase immune function. Grateful individuals tend to have higher levels of immune-enhancing antibodies, making them more resilient to illnesses and infections.

Client Story: Amina's Gratitude Journey

Anita, a 29-year-old artist, came to me overwhelmed by an autoimmune condition that left her drained and disconnected. "I feel like my body is punishing me," she said quietly, her hands curled into her sleeves. "Everything hurts. I don't know how to feel like myself again."

She had tried everything: medication, diet changes, supplements but nothing seemed to help. Emotionally, she was running on empty. Her focus was entirely on her pain, and understandably so.

One day, I gently asked her, "Can we try something different-not to fix your pain, but to reconnect with your strength?"

I introduced her to **the practice of gratitude**. At first, she resisted. "What's the point?" she asked. "How can being thankful change my illness?"

But she agreed to try. She began by writing down three small things she appreciated each morning, no pressure to be profound. Some days it was "the softness of my blanket," or "the way my dog looks at me."

Over time, something shifted. She smiled more. Her art returned. She said, "I'm starting to feel like I'm living with my body, not fighting against it."

Her symptoms didn't disappear overnight, but her relationship with her illness transformed. She began focusing on her **creative gifts**, the support around her, and moments of joy she had once overlooked.

"I still have bad days," Anita said, "but I also have better ones. And I truly believe that gratitude brought me back to myself."

How to Cultivate Gratitude

Here are some practices that can help you harness the power of gratitude for your health:

1. **Keep a Gratitude Journal**: Every day, write down three things you are grateful for. These can be simple moments, like a warm cup of tea or a meaningful conversation.
2. **Practice Mindfulness**: Take a few moments each day to reflect on your surroundings and appreciate the present moment. Notice the beauty of nature, the kindness of others, or the small blessings that often go unnoticed.
3. **Gratitude Letters**: Write a letter to someone who has made a positive impact on your life. Express your gratitude and share how their actions have affected you.
4. **Gratitude Meditation**: Incorporate gratitude into your meditation practice by silently repeating things you're thankful for. Let the feelings of gratitude fill your heart and radiate through your body.
5. **Be Present in Your Relationships**: Take time to express gratitude to the people around you. Whether through words, actions, or small gestures, showing appreciation strengthens your connection and fosters positive energy.

The Biological Mechanism of Gratitude

The impact of gratitude is not just emotional, it's physiological. Gratitude activates the prefrontal cortex, the part of the brain responsible for higher thought processes, and the ventromedial prefrontal cortex, which regulates emotions and decision-making. In doing so, gratitude helps the brain process stress more efficiently, reducing negative emotional states like anxiety and depression. Gratitude works because it connects us to ourselves, to others, and to something greater than our struggles. It reminds us that we are not alone. That in the messiness of life, there is still beauty. There is still hope.

Biologically, gratitude enhances the prefrontal cortex and ventromedial prefrontal cortex-areas responsible for emotional regulation and perspective.

This neuroplastic shift rewires the brain, creating more pathways for joy, trust, and peace.

Emotionally, gratitude creates resilience. Spiritually, it nurtures grace. Physically, it restores balance.

Furthermore, gratitude enhances the production of the "feel-good" chemicals-dopamine and serotonin. These neurotransmitters play a crucial role in mood regulation and overall happiness. When you practice gratitude, you're literally boosting your brain's capacity to feel pleasure and contentment.

Final Thoughts

Our hands tell stories of effort, of generosity, of connection. When clenched, they symbolize resistance. But when opened in gratitude, they become channels of healing. They give. They receive. They touch and transform.

As you read this, take a moment to look at your own hands. What have they held? What pain have they endured? What beauty have they created?

Gratitude allows you to hold your past with compassion and your present with hope. Gratitude is more than a fleeting emotion; it's a life-changing force that can heal the body and mind. It shifts our perspective, strengthens our immunity, and improves our heart and lungs. It is a reminder that even in the midst of pain or difficulty, there is always something to be grateful for, something that can help us to heal.

In the next chapter, we'll delve into the role of the eyes in emotional health and explore how our vision of the world shapes our internal state. Through the stories of those who've gained clarity, we'll learn how the eyes are not just windows to the soul but powerful tools of healing.

Chapter 8:

The Eyes and Our Perception of the World

The Eyes: Windows to the Soul and the Heart of Our Emotions

The eyes are often referred to as the windows to the soul, and rightly so. They reveal much more than just what we see; they also reflect how we perceive the world around us, the emotions we hold inside, and even the state of our emotional well-being. Just as our eyes convey our deepest thoughts, they are also profoundly impacted by our internal emotional state. When we look at the world with eyes clouded by stress, fear, or unresolved emotions, our vision and our health suffer.

When emotions like fear, sadness, or anger dominate our internal landscape, our eyes react in subtle but significant ways. For example, when we're stressed or anxious, the muscles around our eyes tighten, leading to dry eyes, eye strain, and even vision problems. Prolonged negative emotional states can lead to physical changes in the eyes, such as reduced clarity of vision, tension headaches, or a general sense of eye fatigue. But just as our eyes reflect our emotional health, they also have the power to heal. By shifting our perceptions and fostering a positive emotional state, we can improve our vision both literally and metaphorically.

A Poem: Through the Eyes of the Heart

Through the lens of our eyes, we see,
A world of both joy and misery.
But it's not what's outside that counts,
It's the view we give ourselves that mounts.

If fear clouds the way, or grief fills the air,
Our sight becomes blurred, lost in despair.
But when we see through eyes full of love,
The world seems kinder, as if blessed from above.

The Connection between Our Eyes and Emotional Health

Our eyes are closely linked to our emotional health. Stress and anxiety often cause us to squint, strain, or rub our eyes, leading to physical discomfort. Long-term stress can cause vision problems, including blurry vision or eye fatigue. But the eyes also reflect the positive shifts in our emotions. When we are at peace, our eyes are more relaxed, and our vision is clear. When we look at the world with eyes filled with love and acceptance, we see the world in a brighter light.

The eyes have an incredible ability to process both the light of the external world and the emotional energy within us. When we are emotionally overwhelmed, we may experience tightness around the eyes, tears that are difficult to control, or a sense of heaviness. Conversely, when we are emotionally balanced, our eyes appear brighter, more focused, and more open to the beauty of the world.

Client Story 1: Maya's Journey from Fear to Clarity

Maya, a 37-year-old writer, came to see me after a series of panic attacks had affected her daily life. She felt trapped by fear, unable to write, and often overwhelmed by the smallest tasks. "I feel like I can't see clearly," she said, her voice tinged with frustration. "Not only in my work but in my life. I just don't know where to go next."

Through our sessions, it became clear that Maya's fear was rooted in childhood trauma and unresolved feelings of inadequacy. Her vision, both figuratively and literally, was clouded by fear. She was so focused on what could go wrong that she couldn't see the possibilities before her.

We worked together to reframe her perspective on life. Instead of focusing on what she feared, Maya began to embrace what she was grateful for: her creativity, her ability to heal, and her potential for growth. She practiced meditation and visualization exercises to help her see beyond the fear and tap into her inner strength.

Over time, Maya's vision improved. Her panic attacks subsided, and she was able to return to her writing with renewed clarity. She even remarked that her physical vision had become sharper, noting that her headaches, which had been frequent, had disappeared. "It's like the fog has lifted," Maya said, smiling. "Not just in my life, but in my eyes."

Client Story 2: Ben's Struggle with Grief and His Road to Recovery

Ben, a 45-year-old executive, came to me struggling with the grief of losing his mother. His eyes were dull, and his posture slumped as he spoke. "I don't know how to move forward. It feels like I can't see anything anymore. My life has lost its color," he confessed.

Ben's grief had caused him to withdraw emotionally and physically. He couldn't see the potential in his future because he was so consumed by the past. His emotional state was reflected in his eyes; his gaze was often distant, and his eyes lacked their usual spark.

Over time, we worked through his grief. I encouraged Ben to connect with the memories of his mother that brought him joy and comfort. We focused on the beauty she had brought to his life and the lessons she had imparted. Slowly, Ben began to open up to the possibility of moving forward.

As Ben worked through his grief and allowed himself to cherish his mother's memory rather than remain stuck in sorrow, he noticed a change. His eyes brightened, his posture improved, and he found himself looking forward to each new day. "It feels like I can see again," he said. "The world isn't as dark as it once   seemed."

The Eyes and Vision: A Reflection of Our Emotional Health

When we examine the connection between the eyes and our emotional health, we see that they not only reflect what's inside but can also guide us toward healing. In many ways, our eyes are a mirror of our perception. How we view the world and ourselves shapes our emotional and physical health.

If your emotional health is struggling, it's not uncommon for your eyes to show signs of distress. You might experience blurry vision, eye strain, or difficulty focusing. These are signs that your emotional state is taking a toll on your body. Conversely, when we address our emotions, engage in healing practices like meditation and self-care, and shift our perceptions toward positivity, our eyes can regain their natural clarity and vibrancy.

Healing Through Perception

1.   **Shift Your Perspective**: If you're feeling emotionally stuck, try to reframe your thoughts. Focus on what's going well in your life. Practice seeing the beauty in everyday moments.
2.   **Meditation and Relaxation**: Practices like meditation and deep breathing can help release tension around the eyes, allowing them to relax and refocus.
3.   **Gratitude**: Just as gratitude heals the body, it can heal your vision. Spend time each day appreciating the positive things around you. The more you practice gratitude, the more you'll shift your perspective to see the world in a clearer, brighter light.
4.   **Address Emotional Blockages**: If you notice recurring eye problems, it may be a sign of unprocessed emotions. Take time to explore these feelings, perhaps with a therapist or through journaling, and work through them.

Final Thoughts

The eyes, as windows to the soul, offer us a unique opportunity to reflect on our emotional health. When we clear our emotional baggage, we clear our vision. By healing our perception of ourselves, of others, and of the world, we can improve both our emotional and physical well-being.

In the next chapter, we will explore the heart, an organ central to both physical and emotional health, and how love, compassion, and forgiveness play vital roles in maintaining its strength and vitality.

Chapter 9:

The Heart: the Source of Love, Compassion, and Healing

The Heart: A Sacred Center of Emotional Wisdom

Among all the organs in the human body, none symbolizes our emotional core quite like the heart. It is more than a physical pump -it is the sacred seat of our deepest emotions. The heart responds to love, to grief, to connection, and to loneliness. It beats faster with excitement, contracts with fear, and aches with loss. It knows things our mind sometimes denies.

Throughout my journey as a psychologist and emotional well-being coach, I've seen again and again how the heart mirrors our emotional truth. And when it carries unresolved pain, the weight can manifest as real, tangible suffering.

The heart does not forget what we bury deep within it. Every betrayal, every unspoken word, every loss -each becomes a quiet echo inside our chest. Yet, just as pain resides in the heart, so does its greatest medicine: love. And when nurtured with forgiveness, gratitude, and compassion, the heart can heal not just itself, but the entire being. The heart is not only impacted by our emotions but also has the profound ability to heal when we nurture and release emotional baggage.

When Emotions Live in the Heart

Negative emotions like resentment, grief, guilt, and suppressed sadness don't just fade away, they settle in the heart like sediment in a riverbed, gradually slowing the flow of energy. In contrast, love, joy, and acceptance help restore the heart's natural rhythm, creating harmony between body and spirit.

Science agrees: prolonged emotional stress increases heart rate, raises blood pressure, and puts us at risk for cardiovascular disease. But the beauty lies in the fact that the opposite is equally true. Positive emotional states reduce stress hormones, lower inflammation, and activate the parasympathetic nervous system to the rest-and-repair mode that allows our bodies to rejuvenate.

Our hearts are more than biological instruments. They are emotional compasses that point us toward healing when we learn to listen.

The heart is the most direct connection between our emotions and our health. Emotions that we hold onto unresolved pain, grudges, and unhealed grief can create emotional blockages. These blockages prevent the free flow of love and compassion, which is essential for healing. By addressing and processing these emotions, we allow the heart to return to its natural state of balance, vitality, and love.

A Poem: The Healing Heart

In chambers deep where silence sighs,
The heart remembers truth and lies.
It holds the pain we try to hide,
And beats with hope we keep inside.

But when we choose to mend the past,
To free the love we locked so fast,
The heart expands, begins to sing,
Releasing joy in everything.

Emotional Baggage and Its Physical Cost

When emotions remain unexpressed, the heart suffers. Tightness in the chest, palpitations, and breathlessness are not just medical issues but emotional signals. Your body may be telling you, "There's something you need to feel, forgive, or let go."

Unprocessed emotions become weight. And this weight doesn't disappear, it compresses the heart, literally and metaphorically, robbing us of the capacity to fully love, to fully live. When emotional trauma is left unprocessed, it can block the heart's natural energy flow, leading to physical symptoms such as heartburn, a racing pulse, or tightness in the chest. These signs are signals from the body that it's time to release the pent-up emotions and start healing.

Let me share two stories that have stayed with me, real-life journeys of healing where the heart's burden was lightened through emotional release.

Sarah's Story: The Silent Scream of a Compassionate Heart

Sarah, a 40-year-old school teacher, was admired by her students for her strength, kindness, and unwavering voice when it came to teaching values like courage, dignity, and standing up for what's right. But behind her warm smile was a heart quietly breaking, a heart that had spent too long carrying what no one else could see.

At home, Sarah's life was a silent contradiction. Her husband, once a man she believed in, had become her biggest source of pain. A deeply narcissistic personality, he wielded emotional manipulation like a weapon. He raised his hand on her more times than she could count. His words tore into her self-worth. His love was absent, his presence oppressive. And yet, Sarah stayed for the sake of their two young children, the only pure love she still felt in that house.

She endured in silence.
 Not because she didn't know better.
 But because she was too emotionally exhausted to fight the war she'd been living for years.

Then, life dealt her one final blow- her mother, her last emotional anchor, died suddenly.

There was no one left to turn to. No one to hold her pain.
 She felt completely alone.
 "I lost the only person who truly knew me," she whispered during our first session, her voice brittle with sorrow.

Sarah came to me not with words, but with symptoms.
 Frequent chest pains. A tightness that made it hard to breathe. Heart palpitations that jolted her awake at night. Panic came in crashing waves.
 And yet, every medical test declared her heart to be healthy.

But Sarah's heart wasn't fine.
 It was breaking under the weight of **years of repressed grief, emotional abuse, and unspoken sorrow**.

As we gently began to explore her story, the layers peeled away-revealing a woman who had never allowed herself to fully grieve her mother. Her grief had been buried beneath survival-raising children, enduring a toxic marriage, and pretending to be "fine" for the sake of everyone else.

She had never had the space to fall apart.
 So instead, her heart carried it all.

"I think I'm losing my mind," she said once, her voice trembling.
 But she wasn't losing her mind.
 She was losing the strength to suppress her truth.

Through our sessions, we discovered that her symptoms weren't just about the recent loss. They were the culmination of *years* of emotional suppression. Her body was now speaking what her mouth couldn't.

We began the delicate work of healing, helping Sarah **feel safe enough to feel again**.

We used deep emotional release tools, heart-healing meditations, and gentle breathwork to open the space for grief to flow. She wrote letters to her mother, cried without shame, and held space for the pain of that little girl inside her who had never known what real protection felt like.

We named what she had endured, not just grief, but **emotional trauma from a psychologically abusive marriage**.
 We called out the truth she had tried to deny:
 Her pain wasn't weakness.
 It was the natural response of a heart that had carried too much for too long.

Slowly, as she gave herself permission to grieve and heal, her symptoms began to shift. The chest pains had reduced. Her anxiety eased. Sleep came more gently. Her voice grew stronger.

And then came the turning point.
 "I stayed all these years because I was afraid to break the home. But I realize now. I was the only one holding it up."

With courage that came from deep within, Sarah began to plan a new life. Not just for herself, but for her children, for the legacy of love she wanted to leave behind.
 She left the marriage. Not in rage. But in self-respect.

Sarah's journey is a living testimony to the wisdom of the heart.
The heart doesn't just love.
It remembers. It holds. It protects. And sometimes, it breaks, so it can be rebuilt with truth and light.

When love is denied, when grief is buried, when emotional pain is silenced, the heart begins to carry the burden-until it simply cannot anymore. But when we honor our grief, feel our pain, and reclaim our power, we begin the process of **emotional alchemy**.

Sarah didn't just survive.
She emerged with a softer heart and stronger wings.

Raj's Story -From a Dying Heart to a Living Soul

Raj was a man everyone admired- kind, intelligent, and deeply loyal. A respected senior lawyer, he spent his days fighting for justice, but at home, his own heart lived under silent imprisonment. He married a narcissistic wife. She always tried to portray him wrongfully, sometimes by silent treatment and other times by guilt-tripping him.

They were married for 25 years.
What began as a hopeful union slowly eroded into emotional torment.

His wife, once loving in appearance, grew cold, bitter, and calculating.
Behind closed doors, she taunted him, insulted him, and belittled his every effort. She whispered poison into the ears of friends and family:
"I'll make him a heartless soul so no one else will ever want him. He'll be 'mine and only mine' and I'll enjoy everything he's earned." She succeeded in making him an emotionally unavailable person for all around. Love can't reach out to him. Raj, the kind-hearted man, began to question himself.
"Maybe I'm not a good husband," he often thought.

He tried harder. He gave more. He stayed silent, hoping his loyalty would one day melt her cruelty.

But love, when it is not returned, when it is weaponized against the giver, begins to decay. He started to find relaxed moments outside, but all in vain.

Years passed.
Raj's emotions began to die.
He became a shadow of the man he once was- no laughter, no dreams, no affection, just routine work and making money for her and family.
He stopped believing in love.
He convinced himself that emotions were a weakness.
"Only logic matters," he told himself.
His heart, once open and warm, closed itself into a fortress.

Without realizing it, Raj had slowly developed narcissistic patterns not born of arrogance, but as a survival strategy. He no longer felt connected to others. He couldn't cry. He didn't feel pain, or joy, or softness. He became emotionally detached even from his only daughter.

The woman he once loved continued to emotionally blackmail him. She manipulated their daughter, painted herself as the victim, and claimed she had sacrificed everything. But the truth was far from it-she had lived comfortably, indulging herself, while Raj trusted her blindly and bore the weight of the entire relationship, emotionally and financially.

When Raj came to the centre, he wasn't seeking help.
He came because of insomnia, erratic heart palpitations, and indigestion.
"I don't feel anything, but my heart is out of control," he said.

But the heart and liver always remember.

What Raj's body revealed was what his mind had long suppressed-*years of emotional betrayal, suppressed grief, and soul-deep loneliness.*

We didn't start with love.
We started with pain.

In our sessions, I asked him to tell the truth, not the one he'd repeated for decades, but the one buried under shame, guilt, and confusion.

He began to write- not legal briefs, but unsent letters. Letters to himself. To his younger self. To the man who believed in love and to the man who had forgotten how to feel.

We practiced heart-based meditations, gentle breathwork, and self-reflection. Slowly, Raj began to see that he had built walls, not because he was flawed but because he had been wounded deeply and repeatedly.

One day, during a guided visualization, something shifted.
Tears he hadn't cried in decades began to flow.
He placed his hand on his chest and whispered,
 "I thought my heart was dead. But it was just numb- protecting me."

That moment was the beginning of his return.

He forgave himself-not for loving, but for abandoning his own emotional truth.

He started showing up differently for his daughter-softly, gently, without fear.

He took back his power-not in anger, but in clarity.

And for the first time in years, he remembered what it felt like to feel human again.

The heart is not just an organ- it is a vessel of memory, emotion, and connection. When betrayed, it closes. When dishonored, it hardens. But it never truly dies.

Raj's journey is a testament to the heart's resilience.
 Even when love is silenced, even when years pass in emotional numbness, the heart waits for a moment of truth, for a breath of honesty, for a chance to feel again.

Healing the heart isn't about forgetting what broke it.
It's about remembering what it means to truly live.

One afternoon, after a meditation session, he looked up with misty eyes and said, "I don't feel the pressure anymore. I feel peace."

Raj didn't just survive.
He healed.
 And in that healing, he found the courage to love again-starting with himself. He found a true loving partner and without judging, he accepts the love for him and for his soul unconditionally.

The Heart's Power to Heal

Healing the heart doesn't happen overnight. It is a journey of softening, of peeling back layers we've built to protect ourselves. But when you begin, you'll find the heart more resilient and more loving than you ever imagined.

There are some ways to begin:

- **Forgive:** Not to excuse, but to release. Forgiveness dissolves emotional blockages and creates space for peace.
- **Express:** Speak your truth. Cry. Write. Sing. Let emotion flow, rather than fossilize.
- **Practice Loving-Kindness:** Daily affirmations of compassion toward yourself and others open the heart chakra and reduce emotional tension.
- **Breathe Deeply:** Breath connects us to the heart. Inhale love, exhale pain. Let breath become a healing rhythm.
- **Meditate on Gratitude:** The more you focus on what warms your heart, the more warmth your heart will give.

Final Thoughts

The heart is not just the muscle that keeps you alive; it is the soul's voice, whispering your deepest truths. When we learn to listen to its pain, we can guide it toward healing. When we fill it with love, we light up not just our own lives, but everyone we touch.

Our journey through the body has shown us how each part holds emotion, how the stomach absorbs fear, how the back carries burdens, how the hands express what we give and receive. But it is the heart that weaves it all together. It is the heart that transforms pain into peace, loss into love.

And now, as we move into the next chapter, we journey from the heart to the magnificent architect of our reality. Just as the heart holds emotion, the mind shapes the world we perceive. Together, they form the powerful union that governs our well-being.

Chapter 10:

The Mind - The Architect of Our Reality

When the Heart and Mind Dance Together, Healing Begins

We often think of the mind as the master planner - the sharp thinker, the logical reasoner, the one who "knows." But the truth is, the mind is much more than that. It is the architect of our inner world, the unseen sculptor that shapes not only how we think but how we feel, how we heal, and how we experience life itself.

Our mind creates the lens through which we interpret everything: success and failure, pain and joy, love and loss. It is not our circumstances, but our thoughts about those circumstances, that shape our reality. What we think becomes what we feel, and what we feel begins to influence how our body functions. This is the beautiful, fragile, and sometimes dangerous link between the mind, emotions, and physical health.

In my years of counseling, one truth has become undeniable: when the mind is at war with the heart, disease follows emotionally, mentally, and physically. But when the mind softens, aligns with the heart, and allows love, acceptance, and compassion to lead, healing begins effortlessly.

On the other hand, when we reframe our thinking, when we change the way we interpret situations and emotions, we can create an environment that promotes healing and well-being. The power to shift our thoughts is the power to rejuvenate our bodies. This chapter explores how we can reframe our minds, align our thoughts with positive emotions, and, ultimately, experience better physical health.

The Inner Conversation: Heart vs. Mind

Imagine for a moment that your heart is speaking softly, whispering, *"Let go... trust... love again..."* But the mind, often louder, jumps in: *"Protect yourself. Be in control. Don't get hurt again."*

This internal tug-of-war is where many of us live. We feel the pull to connect, to trust, to forgive, but then the mind, shaped by past hurts or ego-based fears, builds walls. When this imbalance grows, something dangerous can happen: we start listening only to the mind and ignoring the wisdom of the heart.

In extreme cases, this can manifest as **narcissistic tendencies** when the mind, out of fear or pain, overcompensates with control, self-importance, or emotional disconnection. The heart closes, not because it is cold, but because it's wounded and unheard. And the mind tries to "protect" us by creating a false sense of superiority, perfection, or detachment.

But here's the truth: **we are not meant to be ruled by our minds alone**. The heart is not weak. It is wise. When we let it guide us with love, empathy, and vulnerability, the mind becomes a tool for growth rather than a weapon of protection. Reframing isn't just about thinking positively; it's about understanding how our thoughts shape our reality and recognizing our power to change them.

The Science of Reframing: How Thoughts Shape Our Health

Reframing, in psychological terms, involves shifting the perspective through which we view a situation, emotion, or thought. When we reframe our thoughts, we effectively change the emotional and physiological response to those thoughts.

For example, consider a stressful situation at work. A person may initially think, "This is overwhelming, I can't handle it," leading to feelings of anxiety, stress, and frustration. This creates a cascade of physiological reactions -an increased heart rate, muscle tension, and shallow breathing. However, if that person reframes the situation, perhaps by thinking, "This is challenging, but I can handle it and learn from it," the emotional response shifts. The body relaxes, the stress subsides, and the person feels empowered rather than overwhelmed.

Reframing also has a profound impact on our physical health. When we change our mental narrative, we activate the parasympathetic nervous system, which helps our body enter a state of relaxation and healing. Reframing allows us to break free from the automatic, negative thought patterns that perpetuate emotional and physical distress.

Reframing: The Bridge Between Chaos and Calm

Reframing is the art of changing the story we tell ourselves. It's not pretending something painful didn't happen, but choosing to see it differently. It's the moment we shift from *"Why did this happen to me?"* to *"What is this teaching me?"*

It's in that shift that healing occurs.

Let me share with you the story of Anna, a vibrant entrepreneur in her 30s, who came to me after months of exhaustion and burnout. Her body was shutting down, but her mind never stopped. She was caught in a cycle of proving herself, of being "enough." Her heart was screaming for rest, for connection, for softness-but her mind kept pushing for more achievement, more control.

When we began working together, Anna cried for the first time in years. Not out of sadness but relief. For the first time, her heart was allowed to speak. We practiced reframing not only her thoughts but her relationship with herself. She began to see that she was worthy without over-performing. That she was enough, simply as she was. Slowly, her body followed. The fatigue lifted. The spark returned.

She said something I'll never forget:
 "I had been living in my head for years. But the moment I dropped into my heart, I started coming alive again."

A Poem: *The Power of Thought*

In the silence of the mind, thoughts arise,
Like birds in the sky, soaring high.
Some are dark, others are bright,
But all have the power to shape our sight.
Reframe the thoughts that bring you down,
And wear the smile, not the frown.
For in your mind lies the key to see,
The world as it was meant to be.

The Emotional Energy of the Mind: Thoughts That Heal or Harm

Just as our body reacts to our emotions, it also responds to our thoughts. The emotional energy created by our thoughts has the power to either uplift or drain us. For example, a thought of gratitude can lift the spirits, activate positive emotions, and rejuvenate the body, while a thought of anger can raise cortisol levels, increase heart rate, and deplete our energy.

When we consciously choose to reframe our thoughts in a positive light, we create an emotional environment that promotes physical healing. Negative thoughts create emotional blockages that disrupt the flow of energy in the body, while positive, constructive thoughts create harmony and balance. The more we practice reframing, the easier it becomes to maintain a positive mindset and align our emotions and physical health with well-being.

The Narcissist Within: When the Mind Silences the Heart

We all carry a little narcissist inside us-not the clinical disorder, but the tendency to protect ourselves with pride, detachment, or superiority when our heart feels threatened.

The mind says:

- *"Don't show weakness."*
- *"You need to win."*
- *"Be better than them."*
- *"Don't trust anyone."*

But underneath those thoughts is often a wounded child, afraid of not being loved.

When the mind becomes too dominant, it builds walls. We become disconnected from others and, more tragically, from ourselves. We mistake strength for isolation, intelligence for control, and protection for self-love.

But self-love is never about ego. It's about alignment.

Healing begins when we notice this imbalance and gently say to our minds:

"You don't need to protect me anymore. My heart is strong. Let's walk together."

Story of Transformation through Mindset Shifts

Jack, a 42-year-old accountant, had been struggling with chronic back pain for years. His pain was often worse during periods of high stress, especially when he felt overwhelmed by work. Jack's initial belief was that his pain was purely physical. However, as we began to explore his emotional well-being, we realized that his back pain was linked to the emotional burdens he had been carrying for years.

Jack had a pattern of thinking that focused on scarcity and lack; he often worried about his finances, job security, and future. This constant worry triggered a cascade of negative emotions, such as anxiety and fear, which created tension in his body, especially in his lower back.

We worked together on reframing Jack's mindset. He began to shift his focus from worry to gratitude, appreciating the abundance in his life, such as his job, family, and health. He also learned to manage his stress through relaxation techniques and mindfulness. Slowly, Jack's back pain began to subside. "I never imagined that my mind had such an impact on my pain," he said. "By changing my thoughts, I've been able to release the tension in my body."

Reclaiming Your Power: Aligning Mind and Heart

When the heart and mind work together, we become powerful creators of our reality. Our thoughts become rooted in truth, not fear. Our emotions become bridges, not barriers. Our physical health becomes a reflection of inner harmony.

Reframing our thoughts can be a powerful tool for rejuvenating our bodies. By shifting negative thought patterns to positive ones, we can reduce stress, enhance our emotional health, and promote physical healing. The more we practice reframing, the more natural it becomes, creating a cycle of positivity that nurtures both mind and body.

Here are some ways to align the mind with the heart:

- **Practice Awareness**: Notice when your mind is running the show. Is it telling stories of fear or love? Judgment or curiosity?
- **Listen to Your Heart**: Place your hand on your chest, breathe deeply, and ask, *"What does my heart need right now?"*

- **Reframe with Compassion**: When a painful thought arises, pause and ask, *"Is there another way to see this with love?"*
- **Choose Vulnerability Over Control**: Open up to love, even when it feels scary. Vulnerability is not weakness - it is the birthplace of connection.
- **Balance Thinking with Feeling**: You don't have to choose one over the other. Let your thoughts inform your decisions, but let your heart lead your life.

Final Thoughts: Choosing Love Over Control

Your mind is brilliant, but it's not always right. Your heart is tender, but it's never weak. Together, they form a compass that points not only toward healing but toward wholeness.

As you continue this journey through emotional alchemy, ask yourself daily:
Am I living from fear or from love?
Am I choosing to protect or to connect?

When we choose love over control, over ego, and over fear-we don't just save ourselves from pain, we return home to ourselves.

The mind is the architect of our reality. When we learn to reframe our thoughts and align them with positive emotions, we create a powerful foundation for healing. The mind, emotions, and physical body are interconnected, and by nurturing one, we nurture all. In the next chapter, we will delve into the importance of self-love and how it serves as the foundation for a healthy body and a balanced life.

Part Two: Nurturing The Self and Releasing the Past

Chapter 11:

Self-Love vs. Selfishness:

Nurturing the Inner Self for True Healing

In a world that often confuses love with indulgence and kindness with weakness, the concept of self-love is frequently misunderstood. Many believe it to be selfishness in disguise, a form of vanity or egotism. But true self-love is neither boastful nor self-serving. It is sacred. It is the soul's whisper that says, *"You matter too."*

The Sacred Ground of Self-Love

Self-love is not about putting yourself above others. It is about placing yourself *among* others with equal value, care, and compassion. It means listening to the quiet cries within, honoring your needs, and tending to your emotional garden with the same love you offer to the world. It's not about isolating or withdrawing but about nourishing your well-being so that you can serve from a place of wholeness. Many people mistake self-love for selfishness, arrogance, or narcissism. However, true self-love is about recognizing and honoring your worth, nurturing your emotional well-being, and understanding that taking care of yourself is not only essential for your own health but also for the well-being of those around you.

On the contrary, selfishness and arrogance stem from avoidance and denial. People who misunderstand self-love may shut themselves off from others' emotions, ignore their own discomforts, and protect themselves from difficult situations. This leads to emotional suppression, which manifests in the body as chronic tension, digestive issues, and liver problems. The liver, in particular, is highly impacted by repressed emotions, anger, and frustration, which often result from ignoring or avoiding emotional conflicts.

When practiced genuinely, self-love becomes the root of healing. It gives you the courage to set healthy boundaries, confront painful emotions, and break patterns of emotional neglect. It invites you to embrace your humanity, not just the light but also the shadows that beg to be seen, held, and healed.

True self-love is humility wrapped in strength. It is gentleness that has walked through storms. It rests in a world that praises burnout.

In this chapter, we will explore the difference between true self-love and selfishness, and how these attitudes affect our emotional and physical health. We will also look at the profound impact that emotional suppression has on the liver and other vital organs.

The Difference between Self-Love and Selfishness

Self-love is an act of kindness towards oneself. It involves recognizing your emotions, honoring your needs, and allowing yourself to feel what you feel without judgment. It's about being kind to yourself, just as you would be to a loved one. Self-love encourages self-awareness, healthy boundaries, and emotional growth. It fosters a sense of worth and self-respect that supports both emotional and physical health. When you love yourself, you nurture your body, mind, and spirit, and in doing so, you are better equipped to offer love and care to others.

In contrast, selfishness is born not from love, but from fear: fear of inadequacy, of vulnerability, of not being in control. It often wears the mask of strength but operates from a place of inner emptiness. The selfish person may dominate, isolate, or dismiss others: not out of arrogance, but from a deep-rooted discomfort with emotional intimacy and vulnerability.

Selfishness rejects discomfort. It avoids conflict. It numbs the heart. In doing so, it creates emotional stagnation, which eventually spills over into the body. Suppressed feelings, especially anger, frustration, and resentment, begin to lodge themselves in vital organs, particularly the **liver**, our body's emotional alchemist.

The liver, as the seat of detoxification, not only cleanses what we eat. It also processes what we feel. When we deny or suppress our emotions, we overload this organ with toxic energy. Over time, this may manifest as chronic fatigue, digestive issues, or even serious liver-related ailments. The body doesn't lie. It remembers everything the heart tries to forget.

A Poem: The Dance Between Love & Ego
Self-love is a quiet river, flowing clear and deep,
Tending to the soul, where old wounds sleep.
It says, "Rest here, beloved, you've done your best."
And wraps the heart in a well-deserved rest.

Selfishness builds walls out of unspoken pain,
It seeks to control, to protect, to gain.
But in the fortress of fear, joy cannot stay,
Only through love does it find its way.

The Impact of Selfishness on the Liver and Other Organs

Our body speaks to us in subtle ways. Our organs are messengers. They speak when words fail. When we experience emotional suppression, our organs are often the first to bear the burden. The liver, in particular, is closely tied to our emotional well-being and it is a sensitive emotional barometer. It holds onto anger that wasn't expressed, frustration that was swallowed, and boundaries that were never set. It is the organ responsible for detoxifying the body, but it is also deeply impacted by the emotions we harbor, especially anger, resentment, and frustration.

When we hold onto unresolved emotions or avoid facing difficult feelings, these negative emotions build up and stagnate in the body. The liver, which is tasked with purging toxins, becomes overloaded with emotional "toxins" that are not processed. Over time, this can lead to physical symptoms such as indigestion, bloating, fatigue, and even more serious liver conditions.

People who tend to suppress their emotions and avoid difficult situations often experience tension in the body, particularly in the digestive system and liver. The emotional stress caused by avoiding discomfort can result in imbalances that affect the smooth functioning of the liver. Similarly, neglecting self-love and engaging in selfish behavior can increase feelings of frustration and anger, which, when unaddressed, can exacerbate liver-related issues.

By contrast, self-love creates a sense of peace and acceptance, which allows the liver and the body as a whole to function optimally. When we take the time to process our emotions, honor our feelings, and cultivate empathy for ourselves and others, we reduce the burden on the liver and encourage the flow of healing energy throughout the body. When we choose self-love, we give our liver the chance to breathe. We stop overloading it with emotional toxins. We allow it to do what it does best - restore and cleanse. When we ignore our emotional truth, the liver retaliates. Not with words, but with discomfort, Pain, Imbalance.

Story of Releasing Emotional Suppression

Emma, a 45-year-old executive, came to me exhausted, not just physically, but emotionally drained. Years of putting everyone else first had worn her down. She suffered from chronic digestive issues, bloating, and fatigue. No medical test could explain her symptoms.

In the discussion, we uncovered layers of emotional suppression. She had always been the giver, the one who never said no, who smiled through pain. Emma had confused love with sacrifice. But inside, resentment brewed. Unexpressed, Unacknowledged.

We introduced her to the idea of self-love-small rituals of acknowledgment, daily journaling, and permission to say no. Over time, her body responded. Her digestion improved, her energy returned, and her heart softened. "For the first time," she told me, "I feel like I'm not invisible to myself."

After a few months of self-love practices, journaling, emotional expression, and learning to confront uncomfortable feelings-Emma's digestive issues began to improve. "I never realized how much I was suppressing," she said. "When I started listening to my feelings and taking care of myself, everything changed."

Aman's Story -The Silent Storm Within

Aman, a 50-year-old self-made entrepreneur, appeared to have it all-luxury cars, a thriving business empire, a sprawling villa, and a reputation for being "unshakeable."

But when he sat across from me, the glow of success didn't reach his eyes.

What did show was the fatigue etched deep into his face, and the quiet distress he could no longer hide.

He had come seeking answers for his persistent fatigue, sluggish digestion, and newly diagnosed fatty liver.
 All the medical reports told him what was happening, but none could explain *why.*

As we began our sessions, Aman confessed he had lived his whole life in *survival mode.*
 Abandoned by his mother at a young age and raised by a stern, emotionally distant father who taught him that tears were for the weak and emotions were a distraction, Aman learned early to armor his heart.

He grew into a man of logic and grit.
 Emotions were luxuries he couldn't afford.
 Anger? Suppressed.
 Sadness? Ignored.
 Love? Conditional.

He believed being in control meant being invulnerable.
 But the truth is- *what the heart buries, the body remembers.*

And Aman's liver had become the container of his unspoken grief, unexpressed rage, and the ache of decades spent pretending everything was fine.

Peeling Back the Armor

Our work together began not with detoxes or diets, but with honesty.
 Aman slowly opened up about the shame he carried-how he felt like a burden as a child, how his father's words, *"Don't be weak like your mother,"* haunted him.
 He had never been allowed to cry, to express, to ask for comfort.

He had built walls so tall, even he couldn't see over them anymore.

As we explored the emotional connection between the liver and suppressed anger, Aman began to realize something profound:
 He hadn't just been suppressing pain.

He had been suppressing love.
Love for himself.

We worked on emotional expression-slow, compassionate journaling, liver-cleansing breathwork, and heart-liver connection meditations.
 He wrote letters to his younger self-apologizing for how harshly he had judged the boy who just wanted to be held.
 He began to soften his internal dialogue, replacing *"Be strong"* with *"Be real."*

He also stopped performing for others- his team, his family, the world- and started asking himself one simple question each morning:
 "What does my soul need today?"

The Shift

One day, Aman sat in silence after a session, eyes closed, hand resting over his heart.
 A tear slipped down his cheek-not of pain, but of relief.
 "I've spent my whole life fighting," he whispered.
 "But maybe, just maybe, I was never meant to fight. I was meant to feel."

Weeks later, his energy improved. His liver enzymes normalized. His sleep deepened.
 But more than the physical changes-it was the emotional transformation that truly marked his healing.
 He smiled more. Hug longer. Said "I love you" to his daughter without hesitation.
 He no longer saw emotions as enemies-but as guides back to his truest self.

Healing the liver isn't just about changing your diet.
 It's about cleansing the emotional toxins, *anger you swallowed, the hurt you denied, the truth you never spoke.*

True **self-love** is not indulgence.
It is the *bravest responsibility* you carry.

It's holding space for your pain without judgment.
It's learning to pause instead of pushing.
It's forgiving yourself for surviving the only way you knew how.

When you treat yourself with gentleness, your body responds with ease.
When you allow the storm within to pass, the sun of peace begins to rise.

Aman's story reminds us that **the liver does not just digest food- it digests life.**
And when you give yourself permission to stop carrying everyone else's expectations, you start living from a place of truth, of softness, of love.

Self-Love is a Responsibility, Not a Luxury

True self-love is not about being self-centered or dismissive of others; it is about nurturing your emotional health, honoring your feelings, and creating space for healing. To love yourself is not to abandon others. It is to meet yourself honestly, hold your pain with grace, and choose peace over performance. It's the kind of love that ripples outward and makes you more empathetic, more connected, more present.

When we confuse self-love with selfishness, we reject one of the most potent healing tools we have. We silence the voice inside that says, *"I deserve to heal."* But when we reclaim self-love, we open the door to balance, harmony, and joy within and around us.

In Closing: Choose Self-Love, Choose Healing

Self-love is not a destination. It is a practice. A sacred commitment to show up for yourself, even when it's hard. Especially when it's hard.

Let this be your reminder:

When you love yourself, you teach your body to trust you.
You invite your liver to let go of old anger.
You give your heart room to breathe.
And you allow your soul to return home.

In the next chapter, we will explore how the art of emotional release clears the energetic and physical residue left behind by suppressed emotions. You will learn how to let go, release, and surrender so that healing doesn't remain a dream but becomes your lived reality.

Chapter 12:

The Path to True Healing

Wisdom from the Bhagavad Gita and Great Thinkers
The Journey to Self-Realization and Healing

In the quest for emotional healing, many of us long for a wisdom that transcends therapy rooms and self-help books: a guidance that touches the soul, not just the mind. True healing isn't just about treating symptoms; it's about awakening. It's about understanding who we truly are beneath the pain, the roles we play, and the stories we carry.

Ancient scriptures like the **Bhagavad Gita** and the powerful teachings of great minds like **Swami Vivekananda** offer us this deeper wisdom. They illuminate a path where the **body, mind, and spirit** move in harmony, a path that doesn't just lead to survival, but to inner peace and radiant health. These teachings emphasize the importance of balancing mind, body, and spirit, showing us how to approach life's challenges with courage, compassion, and a sense of purpose.

In this chapter, we'll journey through timeless teachings that help us rise above emotional suffering, connect with our higher self, and discover the sacred link between emotional balance and physical vitality.

The Bhagavad Gita: A Guide to Emotional Mastery and Inner Peace

The **Bhagavad Gita**, revered for its spiritual brilliance, unfolds as a divine conversation between Lord Krishna and the warrior Arjuna, set on the brink of battle. Yet the battlefield is not just external, it is symbolic of the emotional wars we fight within: doubt, fear, sorrow, guilt, and indecision.

One of the Gita's most profound teachings is **non-attachment**-engaging fully with life without being emotionally enslaved by the outcomes. Krishna teaches Arjuna to act with intention, but without expectation, reminding him that peace is born not in control, but in surrender. This mindset fosters emotional resilience, allowing us to navigate life's challenges without becoming overwhelmed by negative emotions such as fear, anger, or anxiety.

In Chapter 2, Verse 47, Krishna says:

"Your right is to perform your duty only, but never to its fruits. Let not the fruits of action be your motive, nor let your attachment be to inaction."

-- Bhagavad Gita 2:47

When we internalize this teaching, we begin to shift. We stop chasing perfection, stop fearing failure, and start living with presence. We release emotional chaos and step into a state of *equanimity* where the mind is calm, the heart is free, and the body begins to heal.

Swami Vivekananda: The Power of the Mind and Self-Empowerment

Swami Vivekananda, a beacon of strength and clarity, taught that true healing is not something we find outside - it is **an awakening within**. He saw the mind not as a battlefield, but as a tool for liberation. His wisdom helps us reclaim our power, reminding us that belief in the self is the first step toward divine connection.

"You cannot believe in God until you believe in yourself."
- Swami Vivekananda

This is more than motivation - it is a healing truth. Until we embrace our inner strength, no practice or prayer can anchor us. **Self-love**, **self-discipline**, and **self-awareness** are not optional on the healing path; they are essential.

"Arise, awake, and stop not until the goal is reached."
-Swami Vivekananda

Healing is not passive. It requires courage. It calls us to rise, even when we're weary. To love ourselves, even when we feel unworthy. To keep walking, even when the road feels endless.

Vivekananda also spoke about the necessity of discipline and self-control in nurturing both mental and physical well-being:

"Arise, awake, and stop not until the goal is reached."
- Swami Vivekananda

This powerful statement calls us to take action toward our own healing. It reminds us that healing is a journey, one that requires dedication and perseverance. When we align our mind and emotions with this determination, we can overcome any obstacles, whether they are emotional wounds or physical challenges.

Both Krishna and Vivekananda remind us that we are not just flesh and blood. We are consciousness, divine energy, sacred light in human form. This realization **that we are not our pain, but the awareness behind it,** is the doorway to profound healing.

"When meditation is mastered, the mind is unwavering, like the flame of a lamp in a windless place."
- Bhagavad Gita 6:19

In stillness, the storm of our emotions begins to quiet. Through **meditation**, we access our true essence, the part of us that is whole, peaceful, and untouched by suffering. Scientific research now affirms what sages taught long ago: meditation lowers blood pressure, reduces stress hormones, improves digestion, and rewires the brain for joy and resilience.

Swami Vivekananda echoed this truth:

"Meditation is the key to controlling the mind and body."

Through regular practice, we learn to witness our emotions instead of being consumed by them. We shift from **reaction** to **reflection**, from emotional chaos to inner coherence. And in that shift, our body finds its rhythm again, healing itself as we release what no longer serves us.

Story of Priya's Transformation Through Self-Realization

Priya, a 40-year-old teacher, came for chronic anxiety and digestive distress. Beneath her physical symptoms was a deep well of unresolved grief over the sudden loss of her father. For years, she had tried to "stay strong," suppressing her emotions under a mask of busyness and duty.

Through our discussion, Priya began a journey of self-connection. She committed to daily meditation, practiced breathwork, and started writing letters to her father gentle way of expressing what she never got to say. As she learned to sit with her pain instead of running from it, something extraordinary happened.

Her anxiety eased. Her digestion improved. And more than that-her heart softened.

"I feel like I've unlocked a part of myself I didn't even know existed," she shared.
 "Now, I don't just survive each day. I live it, with presence and peace."

Journey of Raj from Suppression to Strength

Raj, a 55-year-old businessman, came with severe hypertension and stress-induced migraines. A high achiever, Raj had always believed that showing emotion was a weakness. Success was his armor. But his body was now crying out for what his heart had long suppressed.

Through mindfulness practices and deep inner work, Raj began to explore the feelings he had buried, fear of failure, a lifelong desire for approval, and the sorrow of distant relationships.

As he began releasing these emotional weights, his physical health responded.
 His blood pressure normalized. The migraines stopped. He felt lighter not just in body, but in soul.

"I thought healing was about fixing something. But now I see that it's about listening. My body was speaking the language my heart had forgotten."

Raj's story is a powerful reminder that emotional healing is an integral part of physical well-being. When we ignore our emotions, we risk damaging our health. But when we embrace self-love, take the time to meditate, and confront our feelings with compassion, we can heal both our minds and bodies.

Bridging Ancient Wisdom and Modern Healing

The Bhagavad Gita and Swami Vivekananda's teachings offer us more than spiritual philosophy; they offer a **roadmap to emotional and physical freedom**.

Their message is clear:

- Heal the heart, and the body will follow.
- Calm the mind, and life becomes clear.
- Know your true self, and suffering loses its grip.

In today's fast-paced, emotionally turbulent world, these timeless teachings are more relevant than ever. They remind us that **healing begins not with doing more, but with being still.** Not with striving harder, but with surrendering deeper.

Let this wisdom be your anchor. Let it guide you back home to yourself.

In the next chapter, we'll explore the **art of emotional release, how** unexpressed emotions get stored in the body, and how letting go is not weakness, but the most courageous act of healing. You'll learn practices to release what you've been holding on to: grief, anger, shame, and make space for joy, lightness, and lasting well-being.

Chapter 13:

The Roots of Emotional Blocks - Uncovering the Past to Heal the Present

Understanding Emotional Blocks and Their Origins

Emotional blocks are like silent walls we build around our hearts. Often formed in response to pain, whether from childhood trauma, broken relationships, or life's heavier moments when these blocks once served as protection. But over time, they become the very barriers that keep us from joy, connection, and growth.

From the perspective of emotional well-being, these blocks are rooted in unresolved emotions like anger, grief, fear, shame, guilt, and often manifest physically in the body. A heavy chest might carry the sorrow of abandonment; tightness in the shoulders might hold unspoken anger. When left unaddressed, these emotional wounds create energetic congestion that can evolve into chronic physical conditions: digestive disorders, migraines, heart issues, and fatigue.

In this chapter, we'll gently explore the emotional roots of these blocks. We'll dive into how early life experiences, painful relationships, and buried emotions become part of our emotional DNA and, most importantly, how we can begin the sacred work of releasing them.

The Impact of Childhood Trauma on Emotional Blocks

Childhood is the soil in which our emotional foundations are laid. When love, safety, or nurturing is absent or when trauma enters our lives through neglect, abuse, or abandonment, then the child within us learns to survive by suppressing emotions. But what is buried is never gone; it simply waits.

The long-term effects of childhood trauma can be profound. For example, a child who grows up with emotionally unavailable parents may develop a belief that they are unworthy of love or affection. This belief can manifest as low self-esteem and an inability to form healthy relationships as an adult. As an adult, this unresolved childhood trauma may lead to feelings of unworthiness, depression, or anxiety, which can block the flow of positive energy and hinder emotional healing. An inner voice whispers doubt. The body holds tension. The heart remains guarded.

Over time, unresolved childhood trauma shows up as emotional blocks and even physical ailments. A person who was constantly criticized may live with anxiety or tension headaches. Someone who endured physical or emotional abuse may carry deep fatigue, back pain, or digestive issues. These are not random symptoms; they are messengers from the body, asking us to listen to the pain we once silenced.

The Role of Past Relationships in Creating Emotional Blocks

Just as childhood shapes our emotional core, relationships in later life often reinforce or deepen emotional wounds. Painful endings, betrayals, unmet needs, or toxic dynamics leave behind residue in our hearts. And when the heart doesn't get a chance to heal, it closes out of fear, not failure.

For example, someone who was cheated on in a previous relationship may struggle with trust issues, even in new relationships. They may feel emotionally closed off, unable to fully open themselves to love and intimacy because the emotional pain from their past is still unresolved. These unresolved emotions may create a block in the heart chakra, preventing them from experiencing love and joy to their fullest potential.

Similarly, a person who has experienced a toxic family dynamic, where love was conditional or boundaries were violated, may develop emotional blocks related to self-worth or fear of rejection. These blocks can have a ripple effect, creating difficulties in current relationships, work environments, and self-esteem. The emotional wounds from these past relationships manifest not just as psychological issues but as physical symptoms, such as headaches, stomach issues, or back pain, all of which signal that the body is carrying unresolved emotional weight.

Other Sources of Emotional Blocks

Apart from childhood trauma and past relationships, there are several other sources of emotional blocks, including:

1.   **Unresolved Grief**: Loss of a loved one, whether through death, separation, or estrangement, can leave deep emotional scars. Unprocessed grief can lead to emotional numbness, sadness, and depression, preventing us from fully experiencing the present moment. If left unhealed, this grief can create a heavy emotional block that affects our physical health.

2.   **Fear of Failure or Success**: A fear of not being good enough or achieving success can create emotional resistance that stops us from pursuing our dreams and goals. This fear can manifest in procrastination, self-doubt, and avoidance of challenges. It often results in physical tension, especially in the stomach and shoulders, as the body responds to the fear of the unknown.

3.   **Guilt and Shame**: Many of us carry guilt or shame for past actions or decisions. This could be related to mistakes we've made or things we feel we should have done differently. These feelings can lead to self-criticism, which in turn affects our confidence and self-worth. Guilt and shame are often stored in the heart and chest area, leading to emotional tightness and discomfort.

4.   **Unmet emotional Needs**: Sometimes, emotional blocks form when our emotional needs have gone unmet for long periods of time. Whether it's love, affection, validation, or recognition, when these needs are consistently ignored or neglected, emotional blocks can form as a defense mechanism. The body reacts to these unmet needs with tension, headaches, or fatigue.

The Process of Uncovering Emotional Blocks

Addressing emotional blocks requires a deep dive into the past, self-reflection, and a willingness to confront painful truths. The process of uncovering these blocks can be difficult, but it is essential for healing. The key steps in this process include:

1.   **Awareness**: The first step is becoming aware of the emotional blocks. This requires paying attention to patterns in your thoughts, feelings, and behaviors. Are there recurring feelings of anger, fear, or sadness that seem disproportionate to the situation at hand? These may be clues that emotional blocks are at play.

2.   **Self-Reflection**: Dive into your personal history not with blame, but with curiosity. Ask, "Where did this belief come from?" or "Whose voice is this in my head?" Journaling, therapy, or guided meditation can help uncover suppressed emotions.

3.   **Emotional Release**: Once the emotional blocks are identified, it's important to allow yourself to feel and release these emotions. This may involve expressing anger, sadness, or grief that has been held inside for years. The goal

is not to dwell on the pain but to allow it to pass through you so that it no longer controls you.

4.   **Forgiveness**: Forgiveness is a critical component of emotional healing. Forgiving others, and most importantly, forgiving yourself, allows you to let go of the past and release the emotional burden you've been carrying. This doesn't mean excusing past behavior, but rather freeing yourself from the negative emotional impact it has on your present life.

5.   **Healing Practices**: Incorporating practices such as meditation, yoga, deep breathing, and energy healing can help clear emotional blocks and promote physical healing. These practices allow the energy to flow freely through the body, releasing trapped emotions and bringing balance to the mind and spirit.

Journey through Childhood Trauma

Sarah, a 34-year-old artist, is feeling emotionally overwhelmed and physically drained. She had suffered childhood abuse, which she had never fully addressed. Despite her talent and success as an artist, she struggled with anxiety, depression, and chronic neck pain. Her body was storing the trauma, and her emotions were constantly in turmoil.

Through our work together, Sarah began to confront her childhood wounds. She learned to express her anger and grief, releasing the emotional weight that had been carried for years. As Sarah began to process her emotions, her neck pain diminished, and her anxiety decreased. "I never realized how much my body was holding onto those old wounds," she said. "Healing emotionally has allowed me to finally let go of the physical pain I was carrying."

Struggle with Past Relationships

Mark, a 42-year-old entrepreneur, had been through a tumultuous divorce that left him emotionally scarred. He carried unresolved feelings of betrayal and guilt, which impacted his ability to trust others. He found it difficult to form new relationships, and his self-esteem had plummeted.

During our discussions, we uncovered that Mark's emotional blocks were tied to his past relationship. He had suppressed his emotions for years to avoid facing the pain of the divorce. Through deep emotional work, Mark was able to forgive his ex-wife and himself, allowing him to heal from the emotional wounds. As he let go of the past, Mark began to open his heart again, building healthier relationships. His physical health also improved. As emotional clarity returned, so did his vitality. The headaches stopped, his energy improved, and his heart slowly opened to love again.

Conclusion: Releasing Emotional Blocks for Lasting Healing

Emotional blocks are not flaws, they are signals. They show us where the heart needs healing, where the inner child is still hurting, and where love has yet to enter. These blocks are not life sentences. With awareness, compassion, and commitment, they can be released.

When we bring light to our shadows, feel what we've feared, and choose forgiveness over resentment, we begin to heal. Not just emotionally but physically, spiritually, wholly.

Let this chapter be your invitation to look inward with courage. The past may have shaped you, but it does not have to define you. Healing begins when you say yes to yourself.

In the next chapter, we will delve deeper into the art of emotional release, exploring various techniques that help clear emotional blockages and restore balance to the body and mind.

Chapter 14:

The Power of Emotional Release - Healing through Expression

"You don't heal by holding it in. You heal by letting it out with love."

Understanding Emotional Release

Emotional release is a crucial aspect of emotional well-being. It is the process of expressing and letting go of stored emotions that may have been suppressed, ignored, or denied. These emotions can be related to past trauma, current stressors, or unexpressed feelings that accumulate over time. When we suppress our emotions, they don't simply disappear; they stay within us, often manifesting in physical symptoms such as pain, fatigue, and illness. In the alchemy of emotional healing, there is one vital process often overlooked yet profoundly transformative, and that is **emotional release**. Like a clogged river that yearns to flow freely, our emotional self too longs for expression. Suppressed feelings, whether grief, anger, heartbreak, or even unspoken joy, do not vanish. They settle within the body, altering its rhythm, its energy, and, over time, its health.

We've seen in earlier chapters how emotions shape our physical being, how love opens the heart, and how the mind constructs reality. But here, we dive into the sacred space of **emotional release**, where expression becomes medicine, and vulnerability becomes power.

Emotional release is not a breakdown; it is a breakthrough. It's not about being weak or dramatic, but rather about **being real**. It is the **soul's way of exhaling**, of saying, *"I can't carry this anymore."*

We often live with a façade-smiling when we're aching inside, holding back tears that are screaming to be shed, choking back words that our hearts have longed to speak. But emotions are energy, and **energy needs motion**. What doesn't move gets stuck, and what gets stuck begins to hurt.

When we deny ourselves the permission to feel, we rob ourselves of the permission to heal.

Whether it's a child burying their pain after a harsh scolding, a spouse swallowing resentment for years, or an adult mourning silently over a lost love-unexpressed emotions sink deep into the body. They manifest as fatigue, tightness, digestive issues, hormonal imbalances, or chronic pain. And often, the **liver** - our body's seat of anger and emotional processing becomes the silent victim.

Love and Expression: The Missing Link

Love is not just a feeling. It is an act of presence. It requires **honesty, expression, and connection**. In relationships, love cannot survive without emotional exchange. Yet many couples fall into a silence that slowly suffocates the relationship, not due to lack of love, but due to lack of emotional expression.

In relationships, particularly in romantic partnerships, emotional expression plays a critical role in fostering intimacy, trust, and connection. Love thrives on open communication and emotional sharing. However, many couples struggle with expressing their true feelings, often due to fear of vulnerability, past hurts, or simply not knowing how to communicate effectively. Fear of judgment, past betrayals, or simply the habit of emotional repression creates a wall between two people who once vowed to walk life together.

"I love you," unspoken, is like a flower left unwatered. Eventually, it withers-not because it wasn't loved, but because it wasn't expressed.

When love is not expressed, either through words or actions, emotional walls begin to form. These walls prevent emotional connection and create distance between partners. In the long term, this emotional disconnect can lead to resentment, frustration, and even physical illness. Love is a healing force, and when it is not given the space to flow freely, it can become a source of stress and tension.

For instance, when partners do not communicate openly about their needs, fears, and desires, these unspoken emotions create a buildup of unresolved feelings. Over time, this emotional blockage leads to physical symptoms such as tension in the body, headaches, digestive problems, or even chronic conditions like liver dysfunction. The liver, in particular, is closely linked to the expression of emotions like anger and frustration. When these emotions are not processed or released, the liver becomes overburdened, leading to physical ailments.

The Unseen Cost of Emotional Suppression in Families

Imagine a home where silence replaces affection. Where parents no longer express love to each other, where children grow up never hearing "I'm proud of you" or "I understand." Outwardly, everything may seem fine: a stable income, shared responsibilities, and family meals. But emotionally, the house is barren.

These are **dysfunctional dynamics rooted in emotional neglect**. Families that stay together physically but drift apart emotionally create environments of silent suffering.

Children raised in such homes often grow up with emotional blocks, mistrust in expressing feelings, and unresolved trauma that shows up in adult relationships. Parents, too, suffer silently, exhausted, unfulfilled, sick yet unaware that the body is simply echoing what the heart has refused to voice.

And often, it is the **liver,** symbolically and physically, that cries out first. Liver imbalances, fatigue, mood swings, and digestive issues are not just health concerns; they are **emotional SOS signals**.

A powerful example of how emotional suppression affects both individuals and families is the dynamic of dysfunctional families. In many cases, families stay together for the sake of the children or because of societal expectations, but emotional communication between family members is minimal. Parents may not express their love for each other or may communicate in a cold, transactional manner. Children may feel neglected, and parents may feel unfulfilled emotionally.

This lack of emotional expression leads to a tense and often toxic environment. The family may continue to live together under the same roof, but the emotional distance between the members grows. Over time, this unresolved emotional tension seeps into the body. The liver, which processes anger and frustration, becomes a common area for emotional distress to manifest. The longer the family members suppress their feelings, the more their physical health deteriorates, resulting in illnesses such as digestive disorders, fatigue, liver damage, or high blood pressure.

In these families, emotional release is almost non-existent. When emotional release is suppressed over time, the body responds with physical symptoms that signal the need for healing. However, if these signals are ignored or not addressed, the emotional blocks only get deeper, making it harder for individuals to heal and reconnect.

From Suppression to Expression: The Healing Bridge

Emotional balance does not mean being happy all the time. It means being honest with how you feel without judgment, without fear. It's about learning to feel, express, and release, so emotions don't pile up like a ticking time bomb.

This expression can take many forms:

- Crying without shame.
- Speaking your truth in love.
- Writing letters you may never send.
- Creating art from your pain.
- Hugging someone tightly.
- Saying "I miss you," "I'm sorry," or "Thank you."

It's not about dramatizing emotions; it's about honoring them.

The Importance of Emotional Balance and Acceptance

Achieving emotional balance is essential for both emotional and physical well-being. Emotional balance involves acknowledging and expressing our feelings in healthy ways, accepting both the positive and negative emotions without judgment. Acceptance is the first step toward emotional release. When we accept our emotions, whether they are uncomfortable or joyful, we allow ourselves to process and release them, freeing ourselves from their grip.

One of the key aspects of emotional release is being able to communicate openly with our loved ones. In relationships, expressing love, gratitude, and even pain can help strengthen bonds and heal emotional wounds. It is through this expression that we create space for love and connection to flourish. Conversely, when we suppress our emotions, we create an emotional imbalance that leads to physical stress and illness. Emotional release is a way to restore harmony within ourselves and in our relationships.

Stories from the Heart: Real People, Real Healing

Story of Journey with Unexpressed Grief

Maria, a 39-year-old teacher, came to me with symptoms of chronic fatigue, anxiety, and frequent stomach issues. After several sessions of deep exploration, we uncovered that Maria had been holding onto grief from the sudden loss of her mother 10 years ago. Despite the passing of time, Maria had never allowed herself to fully grieve, believing that she needed to "stay strong" for her family.

As a result, her body had begun to reflect her emotional suppression. The grief had settled in her stomach, causing digestive problems, and her constant anxiety was affecting her energy levels. Through emotional release techniques, Maria began to express her grief, allowing herself to cry, talk about her mother, and process the emotions she had long suppressed.

In time, Maria noticed a significant improvement in her physical health. Her stomach issues diminished, and her energy returned. More importantly, she felt a deep sense of emotional relief and connection to her mother. "Releasing my grief was like lifting a weight off my chest," Maria said. "I never realized how much I was holding onto until I allowed myself to feel and express it."

Expression Is Medicine

What we express, we release. What we release, we heal. Emotional release is not just a psychological concept, it's **soulful medicine**.

It clears the clutter of past pain. It breaks the generational cycle of silence. It transforms relationships. And most importantly, it brings you back to **you**-raw, real, and radiant.

A Gentle Invitation

If your heart is carrying unspoken words…

If your body is aching from suppressed emotion…

If your relationships are starving for connection…

Then let this chapter be your invitation to **speak**, to **feel**, to **express**, and to **heal**.

Because in the end, emotional alchemy is not about avoiding pain. It's about **transmuting it into love**.

Dysfunctional families or couples who remain emotionally distant may be doing more harm than good to themselves and their loved ones. Suppressed emotions accumulate in the body, leading to physical illnesses such as liver dysfunction, digestive issues, and chronic pain. The key to healing is emotional balance-learning to express emotions openly and without fear, and accepting them as part of our human experience.

By embracing emotional release, we can restore balance to our emotions and our bodies, leading to healthier, more fulfilling lives. In the next chapter, we will explore specific techniques for emotional release and how you can incorporate them into your daily life for long-term healing and growth.

Chapter 15:

The Liver and Emotions - Healing through Emotional Release

In the previous chapters, we explored how different emotions manifest in various parts of the body; how fear impacts the gut, how anger affects the stomach, and how love heals the lungs. Now, we turn our attention to the liver, a critical organ that plays a key role not only in detoxifying the body but also in processing the emotional burdens we carry. Our liver is deeply impacted by the emotions we suppress, particularly anger, frustration, and resentment. If left unaddressed, these emotions can create blockages that not only affect our emotional well-being but also manifest as physical ailments. The liver is more than a detox organ. It's the emotional alchemist of the body-processing not only physical toxins but the deep, unspoken emotions we carry, especially **anger, resentment, and suppressed frustration**.

In traditional Eastern medicine, the liver is considered the seat of repressed emotions. When these energies aren't released, they create internal heat, tension, and eventually disease.

Every grudge held. Every betrayal unspoken. Every time we said "I'm fine" while holding back rage, our liver was listening.

How Emotional Suppression Damages the Liver

The liver is responsible for filtering out toxins and helping our body process nutrients, but it is also the organ that stores negative emotions such as anger, frustration, and resentment. These emotions are naturally tied to our experiences of **repression** and **bottling up unresolved feelings**, often from the past. In my practice as an emotional well-being coach, I've witnessed how people carry emotional baggage for years, often from childhood or past relationships, without realizing its deep impact on their physical health.

When we hold on to these unprocessed emotions, the liver becomes overburdened, and it struggles to detoxify not just the physical toxins but also the emotional ones. This emotional stagnation in the liver can lead to a range of symptoms, including digestive issues, irritability, chronic fatigue, and even liver disease over time. Much like other organs we've discussed, the liver is not immune to the effects of emotional suppression.

Just as the heart suffers in silence, the liver becomes burdened when we:

- **Suppress anger** instead of expressing it safely
- **Harbor resentment** instead of forgiving
- **Internalize blame or guilt** from past wounds

Over time, this emotional toxicity becomes physical: fatigue, bloating, indigestion, irritability, skin issues, and eventually liver dysfunction.

This is not a metaphor. It's **emotional anatomy.**

How Anger and Resentment Affect the Liver

1.   **Anger and Frustration**: Chronic anger, particularly when it is unexpressed, becomes toxic. The liver, as the body's filter, struggles to process this unresolved frustration. Over time, this emotional buildup can lead to irritability, digestive issues, headaches, and a general sense of emotional disconnection.
2.   **Resentment and Bitterness**: Unresolved resentment and bitterness also accumulate in the liver. These emotions often come from past hurts or betrayals and, if not processed, fester and build. The liver stores these emotions like toxins, leading to emotional numbness and physical discomfort, such as liver pain or digestive disturbances.
3.   **Unhealed Grief and Unforgiveness**: Many individuals harbor grief, which, when unaddressed, can add to the emotional load on the liver. Grief that is held in, particularly from childhood trauma or relational wounds, keeps us stuck in an emotional loop. Without forgiveness or release, this emotional baggage results in tension and physical symptoms.

Healing the Liver Through Emotional Release

As we discussed in earlier chapters, the practice of emotional release, whether through expressing anger, forgiving past hurts, or confronting unresolved grief-is a crucial part of emotional healing. It's no different when it comes to the liver. Releasing these emotions allows the liver to function optimally, as it is no longer burdened with repressed feelings.

Emotional Release Techniques for Liver Health
To support the liver in its detoxification, we need to actively engage in emotional release. Some of the most effective techniques include:

- **Journaling**: Writing down your feelings-particularly your anger, frustration, and resentment, helps you process them and release their grip on your liver. Journaling offers a safe space to confront painful emotions and release their hold on your body. Write your truth-uncensored. Let the anger, hurt, and frustration spill onto the page. This is not for anyone else. It's for your healing.
- **Forgiveness as Freedom**: Forgiveness doesn't mean approval; it means **release**. When we forgive others or ourselves, we remove emotional debris from our liver.
- **Breathwork and Meditation**: Breathing deeply is a natural release of emotional tension. With each exhale, imagine letting go of resentment. Let your breath cleanse you.

- **Mindful Expression of Anger**: Learning to express anger in a healthy, controlled way helps to prevent it from accumulating in the liver. This could involve engaging in physical activities like exercise or finding ways to communicate anger constructively in relationships. Scream into a pillow. Hit a punching bag. Talk to someone. Do what you need to do **safely**, to let anger move **through** you instead of staying **in** you.

Dysfunctional Relationships and Liver Health

One of the most significant sources of emotional blockage in the liver comes from dysfunctional relationships, whether they be family dynamics or romantic partnerships. Many individuals suppress their emotions in relationships to avoid conflict or to "keep the peace." However, over time, this emotional suppression begins to take its toll on both mental and physical health.

Example: Clara's Struggle with Family Resentment

Clara, a 42-year-old marketing executive, had spent much of her life suppressing anger towards her parents, who had been emotionally distant during her childhood. Over the years, Clara's health began to deteriorate. She struggled with chronic fatigue, bloating, and digestive issues, and despite seeing several specialists, no physical cause could be pinpointed. Through emotional coaching, Clara realized that her unresolved anger was trapped in her liver.

By confronting her feelings, expressing her anger through journaling, and eventually forgiving her parents, Clara was able to release the emotional burden. Over time, her digestive issues cleared, and her energy levels returned. "I didn't realize how much of my physical pain was connected to emotional baggage," Clara shared.

Conclusion: Conclusion: The Liver Remembers What We Forget

The liver doesn't forget. It holds the echoes of our unspoken truths, waiting for us to listen.

If we want to be healthy, not just physically but emotionally, we must release what we no longer need to carry. Our anger. Our grief. Our silence.

When the liver is unburdened, the body sings again. Energy returns. Digestion eases. And a deep emotional peace settles in. The liver plays a crucial role not only in detoxifying the body but also in filtering out emotional toxins. Anger, frustration, resentment, and unhealed grief accumulate in the liver, causing both emotional and physical imbalance. By actively releasing these emotions, whether through journaling, forgiveness, breathwork, or mindful expression, we can restore balance to both the liver and our overall well-being.

As we've seen in the stories of Clara and Mark, and Jane, when we allow ourselves to confront and express our emotions, we support the liver in its natural detoxification process. This emotional release leads to both physical and emotional healing, enabling us to live more vibrant and healthy lives.

In the next chapter, we'll explore how cultivating emotional balance and mind-body awareness leads to lasting healing, peace, and the return to our truest selves.

Part Three: Rebuilding Emotional Harmony

Chapter 16:

Emotional Balance: The Key to Rejuvenating Your Mind, Body, and Soul

Life should not be viewed for the absence of challenges, but rather for the presence of emotional strength, no matter what challenge you are thrown into.

In this book, we've journeyed through the profound connection between our emotions and our body's health. We've learned how unresolved emotions can manifest in various organs, leading to physical discomfort, disease, and emotional distress. We've discovered that releasing emotional blockages, through expression, forgiveness, and self-awareness, can help restore balance, not only in our minds but in our bodies as well.

Now, we arrive at the most crucial step: **emotional balance**. It is not enough to simply release the negative emotions that weigh us down. To achieve true well-being, we must cultivate balance, the kind of balance that allows us to experience the full range of emotions without letting any one of them dominate. In this chapter, we will explore how emotional balance is the key to rejuvenating both mind and body and how you can cultivate this balance in your daily life.

In the vast orchestra of human experience, emotions are the music of the soul. Some notes are high with joy and passion; others are low with grief or pain. But when all emotions are acknowledged, honored, and integrated, they create **emotional harmony, a symphony** that nourishes your mind, body, and soul.

Emotional balance is not about always being happy. It is about **being aware, being honest, and being kind to yourself** in the midst of every emotional wave. It is the sacred art of feeling fully without drowning, of navigating storms without losing the anchor within.

Why Emotional Balance Matters?

Emotional balance is the ability to **process emotions without allowing them to overwhelm or consume us**. It is about **self-regulation**, which means being aware of your emotional state, accepting it without judgment, and making conscious choices on how to respond. This practice creates emotional stability, which is vital for maintaining both mental clarity and physical health.

Unprocessed or suppressed emotions don't disappear; they settle deep within the body, creating blockages that manifest as:

- Chronic fatigue
- Physical pain or illness
- Anxiety and depression
- Restlessness or insomnia
- Disconnection from the self and others

On the other hand, emotional balance leads to:

- Clear thinking and strong decision-making
- Enhanced immunity and energy flow
- Inner peace and resilience
- Vibrant relationships
- A sense of spiritual alignment

The Mind, Body, Emotion Connection

Our emotions directly affect our biology. When we live in fear or sadness, our body becomes tense, our hormones shift, and our nervous system remains on alert. But when we cultivate emotional clarity and inner calm, the body relaxes, cells regenerate, and healing begins.

Think of your body as a garden. Emotions are the weather.

Too much sun burns, too much rain floods, but the right balance brings lush growth. Your emotional balance is the perfect climate for your inner ecosystem to thrive.

When our emotions are out of balance, our bodies reflect that imbalance. We've already seen how unprocessed emotions affect the liver, lungs, gut, and other organs. But when we maintain emotional balance, we allow our body to function optimally. We allow ourselves to heal, to regenerate, and to thrive.

Here are some ways emotional balance directly impacts physical health:

- **Stronger Immunity**: When we are balanced emotionally, we experience less stress. Stress is one of the greatest contributors to physical illness, as it weakens the immune system. Emotional balance reduces the intensity of stress, helping the body to recover and heal.
- **Better Sleep**: Unresolved emotions can lead to insomnia and restlessness. Emotional balance allows us to manage anxiety and stress, which leads to better, more restorative sleep.
- **Improved Digestion**: Stress and negative emotions are often the culprits behind digestive issues. By maintaining emotional equilibrium, we give our digestive system a chance to work without interference from emotional stress.
- **Increased Energy**: When our emotions are in balance, we experience less mental and physical fatigue. We are better able to conserve our energy, use it effectively, and avoid the exhaustion that comes with emotional turmoil.

Recognizing Emotional Imbalance

You may be emotionally out of balance if you experience:

- Overreaction to small things
- Frequent mood swings
- Feeling numb or disconnected
- Constant self-doubt or overthinking
- Inability to enjoy or be present

These are not weaknesses. They are signals to your soul's gentle whispers -saying, "Come back to yourself."

Healing Through Awareness and Acceptance

The first step to emotional balance is not to fix or force your emotions. It is to witness them with compassion. Let each feeling rise and fall like a wave, knowing that every emotion carries a message.

Ask yourself:

- What am I feeling right now?
- Where do I feel it in my body?
- What is this emotion trying to teach me?

When you allow your emotions to exist without judgment, they lose their power to control you and begin to release their healing gift.

Cultivating Emotional Balance: The Path to Transformation

Achieving emotional balance is not something that happens overnight. It requires conscious effort, practice, and a willingness to change. As an emotional well-being coach, I've seen firsthand how small, intentional changes can create significant transformations in people's lives.

Here are some practices to help cultivate emotional balance:

1.   **Mindful Awareness**: Begin by becoming more aware of your emotional responses. Pay attention to how your body reacts when you feel anxious, angry, sad, or joyful. Notice where you hold tension in your body and take a moment to breathe deeply into that space. This awareness helps you gain control over your emotional responses rather than allowing emotions to take control of you.
2.   **Self-Compassion**: Balance starts with kindness toward yourself. Accept your emotions without judgment, whether they are positive or negative. Practice speaking to yourself as you would to a loved one; gently, with compassion, and without criticism. This self-compassion will create a solid foundation for emotional balance.
3.   **Healthy Emotional Expression**: We've discussed the importance of expressing emotions throughout this book. Balanced emotional expression is crucial. If you're feeling anger or sadness, find healthy outlets to release them; whether through journaling, talking to a trusted friend, or engaging in creative

activities like painting or music. Suppressing emotions will only lead to imbalance, so give yourself permission to feel and express them.

4. **Develop Emotional Resilience**: Resilience is the ability to bounce back from challenges. Developing emotional resilience means learning how to manage adversity without being consumed by it. Cultivate a positive mindset, practice gratitude, and surround yourself with supportive people who encourage you to stay balanced in difficult times.

5. **Create Boundaries**: Emotional balance is about setting healthy boundaries. Whether it's in relationships, work, or personal life, make sure you are protecting your emotional well-being by saying "no" when needed and creating space for self-care. You are not responsible for everyone's emotions; your own emotional health comes first.

6. **Movement and Expression**

Dance, walk, stretch, cry. Let your body express what words cannot.

7. **Mindfulness and Meditation**

Silence reveals what noise hides. Sit with yourself. Observe without reacting. Be present.

8. **Forgiveness and Letting Go**

Unforgiveness is emotional weight. Set yourself free. Let go of what no longer serves you.

Story: Sarah's Journey to Emotional Balance

Sarah had spent most of her life suppressing her emotions. Raised in a household where expressing feelings was seen as weakness, Sarah learned to bottle everything up. Over time, this emotional repression began to take a toll on her health. She struggled with chronic migraines, digestive issues, and severe anxiety.

One day, after a particularly stressful work meeting, Sarah found herself feeling overwhelmed with frustration. For the first time in years, she allowed herself to fully feel the anger and sadness she had been carrying. She sat in her car, closed her eyes, and began to breathe deeply, letting the emotions wash over her. The relief she felt afterward was profound.

"I had no idea how much I was holding in," Sarah said. "Once I started acknowledging my emotions, I could finally begin to heal; not just emotionally, but physically."

Sarah's journey toward emotional balance wasn't easy, but it was transformative. As she began practicing mindfulness, setting healthy boundaries, and expressing her emotions, she noticed a significant reduction in her physical symptoms. The migraines lessened, her digestion improved, and her anxiety eased.

Poem: The Dance of Emotions

Emotions are the waves of the sea,
They come and go, wild and free.
But within their rhythm, there's a dance,
A balance, a grace, a second chance.
When anger rises, let it be known,
Don't let it fester, don't let it grow.
Breathe through the storm, let it subside,
Feel it fully, then let it slide.
Sadness may visit, and joy may soar,
But balance is what we're searching for.
In the quiet moments, in the breath we take,
We find the peace, the calm we make.
So dance with your feelings, and let them flow,
In their release, you'll learn and grow.
For the body and soul, in balance, will thrive,
Emotional health will help you survive.

Affirmations for Emotional Harmony

Repeat these to yourself daily:

I honor all my emotions without judgment.
I allow myself to feel, release, and heal.
I am safe to be vulnerable.
Every breath brings me closer to peace.
My emotions guide me, they do not define me.
Balance lives within me.

Conclusion: The Alchemy of Emotional Balance

Emotional balance is not a destination, it is a daily choice. A conscious return to yourself.

When your emotions are in harmony, your energy flows freely. Your body feels renewed, your heart feels safe, and your soul feels whole. You don't need to be perfect, you need to be present.

Emotional balance is the cornerstone of both mental and physical well-being. It allows us to experience life's ups and downs without being overwhelmed by them. By acknowledging our emotions, expressing them in healthy ways, and practicing self-compassion, we can restore balance within ourselves.

In the next chapter, we'll explore the most powerful healer of all-**True Love** and how it nourishes the roots of your being, opening the gates to deep, lasting transformation.

Chapter 17:

The Power of True Love - Healing Your Mind, Body, and Soul

As we continue exploring the intricate relationship between emotions and health, one emotion rises above all in its ability to transform, restore, and rejuvenate - **True Love**.

True love is not limited to romantic affection. It is the universal energy that flows from a mother to her child, a friend to a friend, a soul to itself. It is the unconditional, accepting, and nurturing force that transcends fear and awakens healing on every level -mental, emotional, physical, and spiritual.

True love acts like a balm for the soul. It encourages us to be vulnerable, to trust, to forgive, and to grow. It has the unique ability to dissolve fears, break down emotional walls, and inspire us to live in alignment with our true selves. In this chapter, we will explore how true love nurtures our emotional and physical well-being, creating a foundation for healing, trust, and joy.

In this chapter, we will delve into how true love becomes a medicine for the soul, a sacred elixir that melts away emotional wounds, builds resilience, and reconnects us to the divine rhythm of life.

True Love: The Universal Healer

True love is presence. It is the moment we look into someone's eyes and feel truly seen. It is the silent acceptance of our flaws and the courageous embrace of our humanity. It says, "You are enough, just as you are."

This kind of love is a sanctuary. It allows us to **breathe**, to **trust**, and to **let go**. In its presence, the nervous system calms, the body softens, and the heart begins to heal. Where fear constricts, love expands. Where pain hardens, love softens. And where illness festers, love brings light.

The Healing Power of True Love

True love is healing because it promotes feelings of acceptance and security. It provides the safety we need to express ourselves fully, without fear of judgment or rejection. In a world where we are constantly striving to meet external expectations, love allows us to be seen for who we truly are-flaws, imperfections, and all. This acceptance creates space for healing, both emotionally and physically.

When we are loved truly and deeply, our body releases oxytocin, the "bonding hormone" that promotes feelings of connection, reduces stress, and supports heart health. Studies have shown that people in loving relationships often experience better immune function, lower blood pressure, and reduced levels of the stress hormone cortisol. Love acts as a shield, protecting us from life's hardships and promoting well-being on a cellular level.

The power of true love also lies in the trust it fosters. Trust is essential for both mental and physical health. When we trust others and, most importantly, trust ourselves, we allow the body to relax and function optimally. Trust enables us to release fear, which is often stored in the body, creating tension and blockages. Love, through its nurturing and supportive energy, helps us to let go of the fear that hinders growth, both emotionally and physically.

How True Love Sparks Well-being and Trust

True love is not just an emotion; it is a source of energy that sparks a profound transformation within us. It sparks:

●   **Self-Love**: True love starts from within. It begins with cultivating a loving and compassionate relationship with ourselves. When we love ourselves, we are more likely to take care of our health, set healthy boundaries, and make choices that nurture our well-being. Self-love reduces feelings of guilt, anxiety, and self-doubt, which can often lead to physical illness when internalized.

●   **Forgiveness**: Love enables forgiveness both for ourselves and others. When we forgive, we release pent-up emotions of anger and resentment that can weigh heavily on our hearts and bodies. Forgiveness is not about excusing harmful behavior; it's about freeing ourselves from the emotional burden that blocks our healing.

●   **Emotional Freedom**: Love helps us experience emotional freedom. It invites us to express our feelings without fear of retribution, creating a safe space for emotional release. By allowing ourselves to feel deeply and express authentically, we can remove emotional blockages that impact our health, such as stress, anxiety, and unresolved grief.

*   **Trust and Vulnerability**: True love encourages trust and vulnerability. Vulnerability is often seen as a weakness, but in reality, it is a sign of emotional strength. It is through vulnerability that we connect deeply with others and ourselves. When we trust ourselves and our loved ones, we release the need to control or hide, which allows our bodies and minds to relax and heal.

How Love Nurtures Health

Scientific research and emotional healing journeys both agree: love is more than a feeling; it is a biological, psychological, and spiritual force. Here's how love heals:

*   **Reduces Stress Hormones**: Love decreases cortisol, the primary stress hormone, and increases oxytocin, the "bonding hormone" that enhances trust, safety, and emotional connection.
*   **Strengthens the Immune System**: People who feel loved and connected experience stronger immune responses, better resistance to illness, and faster healing times.
*   **Improves Heart Health**: Love lowers blood pressure, eases heart palpitations, and reduces the risk of cardiovascular disease.
*   **Supports Pain Relief**: Physical touch, emotional closeness, and even the memory of love can release endorphins, our body's natural painkillers.
*   **Promotes Emotional Freedom**: True love gives us the freedom to express, to cry, to laugh, to forgive, and most importantly, to be vulnerable without fear.

The Gateway to Healing: Love and Vulnerability

Many of us have built emotional walls out of past wounds - walls we thought would protect us, but have only kept us from experiencing true connection.

True love gently invites us to **take off the armor**. It teaches us that vulnerability is not weakness, but strength in its purest form. In that raw, unguarded state, we become real. We become whole. And wholeness is where healing begins.

The Body's Response to Love

When we experience love, whether through romantic relationships, family bonds, or friendship-our body responds in remarkable ways:

1.   **Heart Health**: Love is often referred to as the greatest healer of the heart. It lowers blood pressure, reduces the risk of heart disease, and improves cardiovascular health. When we experience love, our body produces **endorphins,** the feel-good hormones that help fight pain, boost mood, and increase feelings of well-being. Love reduces the risk of anxiety and depression, both of which are often linked to heart problems.

2.   **Immune System**: People who are in loving relationships tend to have stronger immune systems. Love boosts the production of **immunoglobulin A,** an antibody that helps protect against illness. Being loved reduces the levels of **cortisol** (the stress hormone) and promotes relaxation, which in turn supports a stronger immune response.

3.   **Stress Reduction**: Love is one of the most powerful stress-relievers. When we are surrounded by love and affection, our bodies relax, cortisol levels decrease, and our hearts calm. We feel safer, more supported, and less threatened by life's challenges. As a result, our physical health improves, and we feel more grounded and centered.

4.   **Endorphin Release**: The act of loving, whether it's through physical touch, kind words, or emotional connection, releases **endorphins** in the brain. These "feel-good" chemicals enhance mood, alleviate pain, and create a sense of euphoria. The more we experience love, the more these positive chemicals circulate in our bodies, creating an uplifting and rejuvenating effect.

Self-Love: The Beginning of All Love

Before we can truly receive love from others, we must first awaken the sacred love within. Self-love is not selfish, rather, it is self-honoring. It means listening to your needs, respecting your boundaries, and nurturing your soul.

Self-love:

- Silences the inner critic
- Releases guilt and shame
- Awakens the desire to care for your body

- Builds emotional resilience
- Opens the heart to joy, forgiveness, and peace

Forgiveness and Love: Two Wings of the Same Bird

Forgiveness is love in action. It liberates both the forgiver and the forgiven. It untangles the emotional knots that bind our energy, freeing us to feel light and alive again.

To forgive is not to condone but to release. To let go of the poison of resentment and allow love to flow where pain once lived.

Story 1: The Healing Power of True Love

Linda had struggled with chronic back pain for years. She had tried various treatments, medications, physical therapy, and even surgery, but nothing seemed to provide lasting relief. It wasn't until she began to open her heart to her partner and allow herself to experience love fully that things started to change.

Linda had always been emotionally guarded. After a difficult divorce, she had closed herself off to love. But as she began to trust again and embrace the love her partner offered, she noticed something extraordinary. Her back pain, which had once been constant, began to fade. She felt lighter, more at ease in her body, and more open to life.

"I realized that my body was holding onto more than just physical tension. "

"It was holding onto years of emotional wounds and fear."

" Love gave me the courage to let go."

"It wasn't just back pain, it was the weight of grief I had never allowed myself to feel. Love gave me the safety to release it." Linda said.

Mark's Journey to Self-Acceptance

Mark had always been the strong one. Stoic. Silent. But beneath the surface, he was battling anxiety and isolation. Meeting Anna changed everything. Her love was gentle yet persistent. She helped him open the door to his own heart.

"The more I trusted her, the more I started trusting myself. I didn't need to be perfect, I just needed to be honest. That's when the healing began."

"I never realized how much love could heal," Mark said. "It wasn't just about the love I received from Anna, it was about the love I finally allowed myself to feel for myself."

Poem: Love, the Light Within

Love is not loud, it's the whispering grace,
That softens the scars time cannot erase.
It lives in a glance, a touch, a tear,
It dissolves the walls built by fear.

It's not bound by condition, nor tethered by pride,
It flows like a river, wild and wide.
When you let it in, from the depths to the skin,
Healing begins, it comes from within.

Conclusion: Love as a Healing Force

True love is a transformative, healing force. It has the power to dissolve emotional blockages, restore trust, and rejuvenate our bodies and minds. Whether it's the love we give to ourselves or the love we share with others, it creates a foundation for health and well-being. True love is the most powerful medicine you will ever know. It doesn't just change your life; it changes your biology, your mindset, your relationships, and your spirit.

Whether it comes from a partner, a friend, a child, or from within, **love invites us to come home to ourselves**. It brings clarity, safety, connection, and peace.

In the next chapter, we will explore another heart-opening emotion, **Gratitude**, and how it magnifies the healing power of love, deepens our connection to the present moment, and brings profound shifts to our emotional and physical well-being.

Chapter 18:

The Power of Positivity - Transforming Your Life from Within

"Change your thoughts, and you change your world." - Norman Vincent Peale

In the journey toward emotional and physical wellness, there is one powerful tool that each of us possesses: **the power of positivity**. Positivity is more than just having a "good attitude"-it is an emotional and mental practice that can lead to profound changes in your body, mind, and spirit. When we embrace positivity, we open the doors to healing, growth, and success, creating a life that is not only healthier but also richer and more fulfilling.

The mind-body connection is deeply intertwined, and what we think, feel, and believe has an enormous impact on our physical health. Positive thoughts and emotions create a ripple effect throughout our bodies, enhancing our immune system, reducing stress, and improving our relationships with others. In this chapter, we will explore how positivity can become the catalyst for lasting change and well-being.

The Science Behind Positivity

Research shows that cultivating a positive mindset is not just about having an optimistic outlook, it's about actively shaping your brain and body to respond to life's challenges in healthy ways. **Positive emotions**, such as love, joy, hope, and gratitude, trigger the release of endorphins and other "feel-good" hormones in the body. These hormones help reduce levels of cortisol (the stress hormone), which can lead to physical illness if left unchecked.

People who practice positivity are often more resilient in the face of adversity. They experience lower levels of chronic stress, better immune function, and enhanced cardiovascular health. Positivity also supports mental clarity and emotional intelligence, allowing us to navigate life's ups and downs with greater ease.

The Energy We Carry Within

Everything in the universe vibrates, and so do we. Our thoughts, emotions, and beliefs carry frequencies that interact with our cells, our organs, and even the people around us. Positivity raises your frequency; it is the language of light, of healing, of hope.

When you shift from fear to love, from scarcity to gratitude, from anger to compassion, your entire biology begins to respond. Cells regenerate. The immune system strengthens. The heart rhythm softens. The nervous system relaxes. This is not magic, it is science. But it feels like magic because it opens doors to a more vibrant life.

The Neuroscience of Positivity: Rewiring the Brain

Neuroscience reveals that our brains are capable of remarkable plasticity; they can be rewired by repeated thoughts and experiences. Positive emotions such as joy, love, compassion, and gratitude release neurotransmitters like dopamine, serotonin, and endorphins, which not only uplift mood but also:

- Reduce inflammation
- Boost immune function
- Lower stress hormones (especially cortisol)
- Improve memory and decision-making
- Enhance sleep and digestion

Every time we focus on a positive thought or experience, we strengthen neural pathways associated with well-being. Over time, positivity becomes not just a mindset but a default state of being.

Positivity and Physical Health

The effects of positivity on physical health are profound. Studies have shown that people who maintain an optimistic outlook tend to live longer, experience less pain, and recover more quickly from illness or surgery. Here's how:

- **Reduced Stress**: Positive thinking can lower levels of the stress hormone cortisol, which, in excess, can cause inflammation in the body, contributing to heart disease, digestive problems, and immune dysfunction. By focusing on positivity, we naturally lower stress and its detrimental effects on our health.

- **Improved Immune Function**: People with a positive outlook on life tend to have stronger immune systems. Their bodies are better equipped to fight off infections, and they experience fewer illnesses than those who are constantly stressed or negative.
- **Better Heart Health**: Positivity has a direct impact on heart health. Optimistic people have a lower risk of heart disease, lower blood pressure, and are less likely to experience heart attacks. Positive emotions promote a calm, relaxed state in the body, which is crucial for maintaining healthy cardiovascular function.
- **Pain Reduction**: Positive emotions can help reduce the perception of pain. People who focus on the positive aspects of their lives are often more resilient in coping with pain, whether it is physical pain from illness or emotional pain from trauma.

Positivity and the Body: A Scientific Miracle

It's no coincidence that the world's longest-living people-the centenarians of Okinawa, Sardinia, and Costa Rica-live with deep social connection, gratitude, and joyful routines. Their health is not just about diet or genes. It's about emotional alchemy.

Reduced Stress Response

Chronic negativity floods the body with stress hormones, weakening immunity, raising blood pressure, and aging the body prematurely. Positivity calms the nervous system and **activates the parasympathetic state**, where healing and regeneration happen.

Stronger Immunity

Positive emotions signal safety to the body, allowing energy to flow toward repair and protection rather than defense. This results in **fewer illnesses, faster recovery, and lower risk of chronic disease**.

Heart Health and Emotional Coherence

Studies from the HeartMath Institute show that emotions like love, appreciation, and joy create *coherent* heart rhythms, promoting optimal cardiovascular function. The heart and brain then synchronize, creating a harmonious state of being.

Pain Perception and Resilience

Positivity doesn't erase pain, but it transforms your relationship to it. People with an optimistic mindset report **lower pain intensity**, faster recovery, and greater emotional resilience through hardships.

The Role of Self-Help in Cultivating Positivity

While positivity is a natural state for some, for others, it requires intentional practice. This is where **self-help** and self-care come into play. Cultivating a positive mindset is not something that happens overnight. It is a process that requires patience, persistence, and consistent effort. Here are some powerful self-help practices that can help you nurture positivity in your life:

1.   **Gratitude Practice**: Gratitude is one of the most powerful tools for cultivating positivity. When we focus on the things we are grateful for, we shift our attention away from what is lacking or negative in our lives. Studies show that keeping a gratitude journal can increase happiness, improve sleep, and enhance overall well-being.
2.   **Affirmations**: Positive affirmations are simple, yet incredibly effective, tools for rewiring the brain. Repeating affirmations such as "I am worthy," "I am healthy," and "I am capable" can help reprogram negative thought patterns and build a foundation of self-confidence and optimism.
3.   **Mindfulness and Meditation**: Practicing mindfulness helps us stay present in the moment and cultivate awareness without judgment. Meditation has been proven to reduce stress, promote emotional balance, and improve physical health. By regularly engaging in mindfulness practices, we train our minds to focus on the present, letting go of worries about the past or future.
4.   **Surrounding Yourself with Positive People**: The energy we absorb from others has a significant impact on our emotional and physical health. Surrounding ourselves with people who uplift, support, and inspire us can help us maintain a positive mindset. Avoid toxic environments and seek relationships that bring joy and positivity into your life.
5.   **Self-Compassion**: Be kind to yourself. Self-compassion involves treating yourself with the same understanding and care as you would a close friend. It's important to forgive yourself for past mistakes, to accept your flaws, and to celebrate your progress. When we are compassionate with ourselves, we open up space for growth and healing.

A Real-Life Story: Sarah's Awakening

Sarah was in her thirties, plagued by depression, fatigue, and mysterious aches. No medical tests could explain her condition. Every morning was a battle to get out of bed. Her life felt like a constant fog.

But one day, while browsing through a bookstore, she stumbled upon a journal titled *"Daily Gratitude."* She bought it, unsure why.

She began writing three things she was grateful for every night. Some days, it was just "my bed" or "a warm cup of tea." But slowly, something shifted. Her thoughts began to soften. Her energy returned. She added affirmations to her mirror and started short morning meditations.

Months passed. Her body began healing. The fog lifted. One day, she looked in the mirror and whispered, **"I love my life."**

"I realized that the key to my healing wasn't just in medications or treatments, it was in changing my mindset," Sarah said. "By choosing positivity, I was able to unlock a level of healing that I never thought was possible."

Sarah's journey is not rare. It is what happens when the heart chooses light, again and again.

A Poem on the Power of Positivity

Positivity is not pretending,
It is remembering the light in the dark.
It is choosing to smile through the tears,
And hearing hope in your heart's spark.

It is waking up and saying "Thank you,"
Even when life feels unsure.
It's loving the journey, not just the joy,
And knowing your soul is pure.

It is grace. It is a strength. It is magic.
It's a seed you plant every day.

And when you tend it with love and truth,
It will blossom in every way.

Positivity and the Emotional Body

Emotions are the language of the soul. And just like the body digests food, the emotional body must digest experiences. Positivity helps metabolize pain and transform wounds into wisdom.

When you say "yes" to life even through tears-you allow light to enter. Positivity doesn't deny pain. It walks with it, holding its hand, whispering, "You're not alone. You will heal. You will rise."

Final Thoughts: Choosing Light Again and Again

The journey of emotional alchemy is not about avoiding pain, it is about transforming it. And one of the greatest transformers is positivity. When you choose to see the beauty in your scars, the lessons in your struggles, and the hope in your heart, you become the healer of your own life.

Let positivity be your compass. Let it guide your words, your actions, your intentions. Let it fill your cells with life and your days with grace.

In the end, it's not about perfect moments; it's about a positive presence, a peaceful heart, and a soul that chooses love over fear, again and again.

Conclusion: Embrace the Power of Positivity

The power of positivity is transformative; it can heal, uplift, and renew both your emotional and physical health. It is not just about thinking positively; it is about actively cultivating a mindset that supports your well-being. By practicing gratitude, affirmations, mindfulness, and self-compassion, you can create a life that is full of joy, love, and healing. **Affirmations to Anchor Positivity**

Repeat them, write them, believe them:

- I am open to all the goodness the universe has for me.

- My body responds to love, joy, and peace.

- I choose positive thoughts that heal and empower me.

- I radiate light, even in the darkest of times.

- My life is unfolding in beautiful and perfect ways.

As you continue your journey, remember that the choice to embrace positivity is yours. It is a tool that can help you overcome challenges, restore balance, and create the vibrant life you deserve.

Chapter 19:

Resilience and Emotional Strength: The Sacred Armor of the Soul

Life, in its essence, is a journey filled with highs and lows. We all face challenges, whether they come in the form of personal loss, illness, heartbreak, or unexpected life changes. However, what truly sets us apart is how we respond to these challenges; this is where **resilience** and **emotional strength** come into play.

Resilience is the ability to adapt and bounce back from adversity, and emotional strength is the foundation upon which resilience is built. Resilience is not about being untouched by pain; it is about being touched and still choosing to rise. Emotional strength is not about suppressing feelings; it is about embracing them with courage, transforming wounds into wisdom.

These two forces are not just survival tools, they are pathways to healing, growth, and ultimately, to a life lived with purpose and soul. In this chapter, we'll explore how resilience and emotional strength deeply influence our physical and emotional well-being, and how we can cultivate them to not just survive but *thrive*. These qualities do not make us immune to pain or hardship; instead, they empower us to face difficulties with grace, endurance, and a sense of purpose.

In this chapter, we will explore the profound connection between emotional strength and physical health, the importance of resilience in overcoming life's challenges, and the key practices that help cultivate these qualities.

The Invisible Bridge: Resilience and the Mind-Body Connection

Every emotion you feel travels through your nervous system, affecting the rhythms of your heart, the state of your immune system, and the chemistry of your brain. The way your body processes stress is not separate from your emotional experience, rather, it is *woven* into it.

When you face a storm-be it a loss, betrayal, illness, or failure, your body enters a stress response. Cortisol rises, your heart races, digestion slows, and immunity weakens. But resilience, the deep inner capacity to recover, acts like a healing balm. It helps your body return to balance. It protects your heart, your cells, your hormones, and your life force.

Resilient people are not immune to stress - they are simply more capable of moving through it without being consumed by it. Resilience is not just a psychological trait; it is deeply rooted in our body's ability to cope with stress and recover from trauma. Resilience, however, helps us manage stress more effectively. When we develop emotional strength and resilience, we are better equipped to handle life's pressures, leading to reduced stress and improved overall health. A resilient person is more likely to have a healthy heart, better immune function, and a lower risk of developing chronic diseases because their emotional strength enables them to process and release stress in healthier ways.

Emotional Strength: The Anchor in the Storm

Emotional strength doesn't mean being emotionally numb or always appearing "strong." In fact, true emotional strength lies in authenticity. It means allowing yourself to feel deeply and still choosing to move forward with grace. It means holding space for your grief *and* your hope. Emotional strength refers to our ability to maintain emotional balance and clarity, even in the face of difficulty. It is about remaining grounded in our values and beliefs while embracing the inevitable challenges of life. Emotional strength allows us to respond to adversity not with fear or anger, but with wisdom, patience, and grace.

Here's how emotional strength contributes to resilience:

1.   **Emotional Regulation**: Instead of reacting from fear, anger, or despair, emotionally strong individuals pause, breathe, and choose conscious responses. They don't let pain define them, they let it shape their wisdom.
2.   **Positive Outlook**: Emotional strength helps us maintain a positive outlook, even in the face of adversity. It's not about ignoring the negative aspects of life but about choosing to focus on solutions, growth, and the lessons that come from hardship.
3.   **Self-Confidence**: People with emotional strength trust in their ability to overcome difficulties. This confidence allows them to face challenges head-on, knowing that they have the internal resources to navigate through tough times.
4.   **Hope-Filled Vision**: Emotional strength fosters a mindset of possibility. Even in dark times, there is an inner whisper that says, "This too shall pass. I will heal."
5.   **Self-Belief**: Emotionally strong people carry a quiet confidence. They may fall, but they trust their ability to rise. This self-belief becomes their compass.

6.   **Openness to Support**: Strength is not solitary. It is the wisdom to ask for help, to lean on love, and to allow community and connection to be part of healing. It's about recognizing that we are not alone in our struggles and that reaching out for support from loved ones, mentors, or professionals is a sign of strength, not weakness.

The Body as a Reflection of Resilience

Chronic stress is the silent saboteur of well-being. But emotional resilience changes the way your body *perceives* and *responds* to stress. Here's how it works:

- **Heart Health**: Resilience reduces inflammation and supports cardiovascular function. Your heart, both emotionally and biologically, benefits from your inner strength.
- **Immune Function**: Resilient individuals experience fewer illnesses and recover faster. Their bodies are not constantly in defense mode, they are in a state of *repair*.
- **Pain Tolerance and Recovery**: Emotional strength allows you to manage pain with more calm and less fear, whether it's physical pain or emotional trauma. It opens space for healing.

Resilience doesn't just help you cope, it helps you *heal faster* and *live longer.*

Building Emotional Strength and Resilience

Resilience is not an innate trait; it is something that can be nurtured and developed over time. You are not born resilient, you *become* resilient. Like any muscle, resilience and emotional strength grow stronger with use. Here are some key practices to help build emotional strength and resilience:

1.   **Mindfulness and Meditation**: Mindfulness helps us stay present and focused, reducing stress and preventing negative emotions from overwhelming us. Meditation has been shown to enhance emotional regulation, lower cortisol levels, and improve overall health.
2.   **Self-Care Practices**: Taking care of your physical, emotional, and mental health is essential for building resilience. Regular exercise, healthy

eating, and sufficient sleep are all key components of self-care that support both emotional and physical well-being.

3.   **Rewriting Inner Dialogue**: The way we speak to ourselves has a profound impact on our emotional strength. Replacing self-criticism with self-compassion helps us stay grounded during difficult times. Practice reframing negative thoughts into empowering statements, such as "I am capable" or "I have the strength to overcome this." Replace "I can't" with "I'm learning." Replace "This is too much" with "I can take this one breath at a time." Your self-talk becomes your soul's script.

4.   **Gratitude**: Gratitude is a powerful tool for building resilience. By focusing on what we are grateful for, we shift our focus away from the difficulties in our lives. Gratitude helps to improve our emotional outlook and enhances our resilience by fostering a sense of hope and optimism. Gratitude opens the heart and fuels hope.

5.   **Human Connection**: Seek the people who remind you of your strength. Let love in. Let support hold you. Resilience often blooms in the garden of community. Social support is a critical factor in building resilience. Surround yourself with people who uplift, encourage, and inspire you. Healthy relationships provide emotional strength during difficult times and remind us that we are not alone.

Real Story: John's Journey from Grief to Grace

John lost his beloved wife of 30 years. In a single moment, his world collapsed. Grief enveloped him. His health declined-appetite, sleep, and energy faded. But one day, as he looked at a photo of her smiling face, something awakened.

He whispered, "She wouldn't want me to disappear. She would want me to *live*." That moment became his turning point.

John started therapy, wrote in his journal every day, practiced breathing exercises, and took daily walks in the park where they once strolled together. Slowly, his physical health returned. His heart still ached, but he had found a deeper strength within a resilience rooted in love, not fear.

"I didn't escape the pain," he said. "I transformed through it. That's what resilience is - loving yourself enough to keep living, even when it hurts."

A Poem on Resilience

Resilience is the strength within,
That helps you rise and start again.
When life knocks you down, don't fear,
Your inner power will appear.
Through every trial, every tear,
You'll find the strength to persevere.
For in the darkest times we see,
The light of hope sets us free.
With each step forward, you'll grow strong,
The resilience to carry on.
For life's challenges, big and small,
Can be overcome, one step at a time, after all.

Conclusion: Rise With Grace, Heal With Power

Resilience and emotional strength are not abstract concepts-they are **sacred companions** on your healing path. They do not deny your pain; they honor it. They do not suppress your emotions; they help you express them wisely. And they do not make you invulnerable; rather, they make you *unstoppable.* Resilience and emotional strength are vital components of our journey toward healing and wellness. They are the keys that allow us to transform adversity into opportunities for growth. By cultivating emotional strength, we not only improve our mental well-being but also enhance our physical health, creating a balanced, empowered life.

As you continue your journey, remember that resilience is within you. It is not the absence of hardship, but the ability to rise above it with grace, hope, and courage. Trust in your ability to heal, grow, and thrive, no matter what life throws your way.

Dear reader, if you are in a storm right now, know this: *You have everything within you to survive, to heal, and to rise.* And if you are thriving now, continue to nourish your emotional strength; it will carry you with grace into whatever life brings next.

Resilience is your soul's way of saying, **"You are meant to bloom-even after the fire."**

Chapter 20:

The Power of Forgiveness - Letting Go of Emotional Baggage

"Forgiveness is not something we do for others. It is something we do for ourselves; to set ourselves free."

In the vast tapestry of emotional healing, forgiveness is the golden thread that binds broken hearts, soothes aching souls, and releases the body from silent suffering. It is not about forgetting the wound, nor excusing the harm done. It is about reclaiming your peace, taking back your power, and choosing love over lingering pain. Forgiveness is not just about letting others off the hook. It is a profound act of healing that frees you from the emotional chains of the past. The burden of unresolved anger, resentment, and regret can create significant emotional and physical blockages that hinder our growth, peace of mind, and overall well-being. In this chapter, we explore how forgiveness is essential to emotional health and how it can dramatically improve your physical health by releasing the negative energy that affects your body.

Emotional Baggage: The Weight We Carry

When we hold on to negative emotions, let it be anger, regret, betrayal, or guilt, we create an energetic imbalance that can manifest as physical symptoms. Our body, mind, and emotions are interconnected, and unresolved emotional wounds affect us on a cellular level. These emotions can create stress, trigger chronic pain, and compromise immune function. Our liver, which processes emotions like anger and frustration, often bears the brunt of this emotional weight. Emotions like anger and bitterness don't just live in our minds. They live in our *bodies*. The liver, often called the seat of suppressed emotions, especially harbors anger and frustration. Chronic resentment can manifest as digestive issues, tension headaches, insomnia, or autoimmune disorders. When emotional baggage lingers, it slowly chips away at our vitality.

Unforgiven hurts linger in the form of toxic emotions, and their effect on the body is profound. Research has shown that people who struggle to forgive tend to have higher blood pressure, increased heart rates, and are more prone to conditions like anxiety and depression. These symptoms are often an outward manifestation of the emotional blocks we carry.

The Healing Power of Forgiveness

Forgiveness is the key that unlocks the door to emotional freedom. When we forgive, we are not excusing the behavior of others; we are liberating ourselves from the ongoing harm caused by our negative emotions. Forgiveness is a gift we give ourselves-allowing us to move forward, heal, and experience life with renewed energy and clarity. It's not a sign of weakness- it's the highest form of strength. When you forgive, you are saying, *"I choose to stop suffering."*

Scientific research confirms this: people who forgive have lower cortisol (stress hormone) levels, healthier blood pressure, improved heart rate variability, and reduced risk of depression and chronic disease. Forgiveness *unblocks* the emotional energy that's been trapped in the body, often resulting in profound physical healing.

Let's be clear: forgiveness is a process, not a one-time event. It's not always easy, especially when we've been deeply hurt. But by embracing forgiveness, we reclaim our peace, happiness, and health.

Why Forgiveness Matters for Your Health

Forgiving others and even ourselves is essential for emotional and physical healing. When we practice forgiveness, we reduce the levels of cortisol (the stress hormone) in our bodies, which in turn helps to lower blood pressure, reduce inflammation, and boost our immune system. These physical benefits are a direct result of the emotional release that comes with forgiveness.

Forgiveness also enhances mental health by fostering emotional resilience. It helps us break the cycle of negativity and resentment that keeps us stuck in the past. It allows us to embrace the present moment with open arms, which is crucial for maintaining emotional balance and clarity.

The Role of Self-Forgiveness

Forgiveness isn't just about letting go of the hurt others have caused. It's also about forgiving ourselves for past mistakes, perceived shortcomings, and decisions we regret. Self-forgiveness is essential for mental health because it allows us to accept ourselves as imperfect human beings.

The act of forgiving ourselves releases guilt and shame-emotions that often weigh us down physically. Just as we extend forgiveness to others, we must also show compassion to ourselves. This helps us foster a sense of inner peace and acceptance, which directly impacts our physical well-being.

The Healing Journey of Emma

Emma came into therapy weighed down by chronic digestive issues, fatigue, and migraines. But what truly ailed her was invisible-anger buried deep since childhood. Her father had left the family when she was 10. Her body had been holding that pain for over two decades.

Through a process of emotional release, mirror work, and guided forgiveness practices, Emma allowed herself to feel and grieve. She didn't forgive to condone her father's actions-she forgave to unshackle herself from years of suffering.

As she released the resentment, something beautiful happened: her symptoms eased. Her body started healing. Her relationships transformed. She began to feel alive again.

Forgiveness and Emotional Freedom

Forgiveness is not a passive act; it is a conscious choice to let go of the negative emotions that hold us back. It's a commitment to releasing what no longer serves us, so we can make room for peace, love, and emotional growth.

In a sense, forgiveness is an act of emotional self-care. It strengthens our emotional resilience and helps us move forward with a sense of clarity and purpose. When we forgive, we align ourselves with the universal flow of love and compassion, which is essential for nurturing our body and mind. Forgiveness is not about denying the pain, it's about transforming it. It's about telling your story from a place of power, not from a place of wounding.

To forgive doesn't mean you accept the behavior. It means you choose to no longer carry the energy of that pain. You choose peace over poison. You choose freedom over control.

How to Cultivate Forgiveness: A Gentle Guide

1.   **Acknowledge the Hurt** - Suppressed emotions don't heal. Honor your pain. Feel it fully.
2.   **Write a Release Letter** - Even if you never send it, write everything you want to express. Burn it afterward as a symbolic release.
3.   **Practice Mirror Work** - Look into your own eyes and say, *"I forgive you. I love you."* Do this daily. Start with yourself.
4.   **Use Guided Meditation** - Visualize sending love and light to the person you need to forgive. See yourself cutting the energetic cord.
5.   **Breathe Through It** - Deep belly breathing calms the nervous system and helps release emotional tension from the body.

Forgiveness Is an Act of Emotional Freedom

Forgiveness does not mean reconciliation. It means *liberation*. It means breaking the chains of emotional slavery and choosing inner peace.

It means aligning yourself with the highest vibration of all: **Love**.

Conclusion: Releasing the Past to Embrace the Future

Forgiveness is one of the most powerful medicines you can offer your heart, your body, and your life. It is not about the other person- it is about *you*. It's about letting go so you can grow. About clearing the space within so love can flourish. The act of forgiveness is a powerful tool for emotional and physical well-being. It is not only a means to heal from past hurt but also an opportunity to cultivate a healthier, more vibrant future. When we forgive, we let go of the emotional baggage that weighs us down, and in doing so, we release the physical tension that manifests as disease.

When you forgive, you step into your true power. You become the alchemist of your healing. And in that transformation, your emotional baggage turns into wings that will carry you to your highest, healthiest, most joyful self.

Forgiveness is a lifelong journey, a continuous practice of healing and growth. It is a testament to our emotional strength and resilience. By embracing forgiveness, we clear the path for emotional and physical well-being, allowing us to fully live in the present moment with love, compassion, and vitality.

Expanded Thoughts on Forgiveness and Health

Forgiveness is more than just a psychological concept; it's an essential part of emotional healing that directly impacts the body. In the next few sections, we will explore practical ways to cultivate forgiveness and offer forgiveness to ourselves and others. These techniques will help you further heal from past wounds and embrace the power of emotional freedom, leading to a more vibrant life.

Chapter 21:

The Role of Boundaries in Emotional Health

Boundaries are an essential yet often overlooked aspect of emotional health. Setting and maintaining healthy boundaries is crucial for protecting our mental, emotional, and physical well-being. Boundaries help us define what is acceptable in our relationships, interactions, and experiences, and more importantly, what is not. In this chapter, we will explore the importance of boundaries in emotional health, how to set them, and the profound impact they can have on your physical well-being.

Understanding Boundaries and Their Importance

A boundary is a limit we set for ourselves in our relationships with others. It's the emotional, mental, and physical space we create to protect our integrity and well-being. Without clear boundaries, we risk overextending ourselves, becoming overwhelmed, and neglecting our own needs.

Imagine a house without walls. If there are no boundaries, the house becomes vulnerable to external threats- rain, wind, or unwanted intruders. Similarly, without emotional boundaries, we are vulnerable to emotional overwhelm, stress, and burnout. Healthy boundaries allow us to preserve our emotional energy, respect ourselves, and maintain our personal well-being.

The inability to set boundaries often stems from a lack of self-awareness or the fear of disappointing others. Many people, especially those who are naturally empathetic, find it difficult to say "no" or establish limits, fearing that they will hurt someone else's feelings or cause conflict. However, what many fail to realize is that by not setting boundaries, they are inadvertently hurting themselves.

How Boundaries Affect Our Emotional Health

Boundaries are an expression of self-respect and self-love. When we set boundaries, we acknowledge our own needs and prioritize our well-being. Boundaries help us create space for self-care and reflection, allowing us to protect ourselves from emotional depletion and stress.

When we consistently violate our own boundaries or allow others to overstep them, we experience a loss of control over our emotional energy. This depletion can manifest in a variety of ways- exhaustion, anxiety, depression, irritability, or even physical ailments like headaches, digestive issues, and chronic fatigue.

In relationships, poor boundaries often lead to resentment, feelings of helplessness, and emotional burnout. When we fail to protect our emotional space, we may begin to feel as though we are constantly giving, without receiving in return. This imbalance creates emotional friction and damages the quality of our connections with others.

The Impact of Boundaries on Physical Health

Just as emotional boundaries protect our mental health, they also play a significant role in preserving our physical well-being. The body and mind are intimately connected, and when our emotional energy is compromised, it can directly impact our physical health. Chronic stress, anxiety, and emotional strain caused by poor boundaries can trigger a variety of health issues, including high blood pressure, heart disease, weakened immune function, and digestive problems.

The liver, for example, is directly affected by unresolved emotions such as anger, frustration, and resentment. These emotions often arise when boundaries are violated, whether by others or by our own inability to assert ourselves. When we hold onto these emotions without releasing them, they accumulate in the body and contribute to physical illness.

By setting healthy boundaries, we protect our emotional energy and, in turn, safeguard our physical health. Boundaries help us manage stress, prevent burnout, and preserve our vitality.

Learning to Set Healthy Boundaries

Setting healthy boundaries requires practice, self-awareness, and the courage to assert your needs. Here are some steps to help you establish and maintain boundaries:

1.   **Know Your Limits**: Understand what is acceptable and what isn't. Reflect on your needs and values to determine what boundaries you need to set.
2.   **Communicate Clearly**: Be assertive but kind when communicating your boundaries. You have the right to say "no" without feeling guilty. Clear communication helps prevent misunderstandings and strengthens relationships.
3.   **Practice Self-Care**: Prioritize your well-being by setting aside time for rest, relaxation, and activities that nourish your body and mind. Remember that self-care is not selfish; it is essential for maintaining emotional and physical health.

4.   **Set Consequences**: If someone repeatedly violates your boundaries, it's important to set consequences. This might mean limiting contact or distancing yourself from the person or situation.

5.   **Seek Support**: Setting boundaries can be difficult, especially if you've been conditioned to please others. Seek support from trusted friends, family, or a therapist who can help you navigate the process.

Story: Emily's Journey to Boundary Setting

Emily had always been the "go-to" person for everyone in her family. Whether it was her siblings, parents, or friends, they all relied on her to help solve their problems and take care of their needs. While Emily was happy to help, she found herself feeling emotionally drained and physically exhausted. Her energy was constantly depleted, and she struggled with chronic headaches and sleep issues.

After attending therapy and learning about the importance of setting boundaries, Emily realized that she had been neglecting her own needs in favor of others. She began to practice saying "no" and creating space for herself, even if it meant disappointing others. Initially, it was uncomfortable, but over time, she began to feel empowered and more balanced. Her headaches diminished, her sleep improved, and her overall sense of well-being flourished.

Emily learned that setting boundaries was not an act of rejection, but an act of self-preservation. By taking care of her own needs, she was able to show up as a more present and compassionate person in her relationships.

Story: John's Struggle with Boundaries in a Toxic Work Environment

John worked in a high-pressure corporate environment where he was expected to be available 24/7. His boss constantly contacted him after hours, and his colleagues would drop work on him without warning. Over time, John felt overwhelmed and stressed, which started to take a toll on his physical health. He developed digestive issues, experienced frequent migraines, and his energy levels plummeted.

John realized that his inability to set boundaries at work was contributing to his physical decline. He started by setting clear limits with his boss and colleagues, ensuring that his personal time was respected. Though it was difficult at first, John gradually regained control over his schedule. His health improved as he learned to assert his needs and prioritize his well-being.

This experience taught John that boundaries are not just essential for emotional health- they are crucial for physical well-being as well.

Conclusion: Embracing Boundaries for a Healthier Life

Boundaries are an essential part of maintaining emotional health and physical well-being. They protect us from emotional depletion, prevent burnout, and ensure that our needs are met. By learning to set and respect our boundaries, we take control of our emotional energy, reduce stress, and promote healing.

Remember, setting boundaries is an act of self-respect. It allows you to create space for self-care, growth, and healing. When you honor your own boundaries, you create healthier relationships, preserve your energy, and safeguard your physical health. Boundaries are not walls-they are bridges that allow us to live authentically and fully in alignment with our true selves.

Part Four:

Love Beyond Fear & Building a New Emotional Legacy

Chapter 22:

Love Without Chains - Healing the Fear of Re-Love and Divorce in Dysfunctional Families

Love is the most powerful force in the universe, but when distorted by fear, guilt, or past trauma, it can become one of the heaviest burdens we carry. In many dysfunctional families, love is not absent; it is often deeply felt, but also tangled in expectations, control, silence, and fear. One of the greatest emotional blocks people face is the **fear of letting go of dysfunctional relationships,** not because they are happy, but because they are afraid of the unknown. They fear the loneliness, the stigma, and the vulnerability that comes with starting over.

This chapter is about **the courage to choose love again** to release the fear of divorce, of remarriage, or of loving again after heartbreak. It's about breaking the cycle of emotional paralysis that dysfunctional systems create, and realizing that **true love is never controlling, fearful, or sacrificing one's soul to maintain appearances.**

The Illusion of Staying "For the Sake of Family"

In many cultures and homes, divorce is not just seen as a breakup- it's treated as a failure, a shameful act, or a betrayal of tradition. People stay in emotionally abusive, toxic, or neglectful relationships for decades, convincing themselves they are doing it "for the children," "for the family," or because "love means sacrifice."

But **what kind of love teaches suppression instead of expression?** What legacy are we leaving for our children when we teach them that love means enduring emotional emptiness or silent suffering?

Children raised in such environments often absorb a confusing message: **love is painful, unpredictable, and filled with unspoken grief.** This becomes their blueprint for future relationships. They learn to tolerate the intolerable. They develop deep emotional blocks- fear of intimacy, fear of abandonment, or fear of rejection.

They carry this baggage into adulthood, and the cycle continues until someone is brave enough to break it.

Emotional Baggage: The Inheritance of Silence

Dysfunctional families pass down **not just behaviors, but emotions**-unspoken pain, hidden fears, repressed desires. These emotional inheritances become our unconscious patterns.

When we suppress our truth for too long, the emotional energy doesn't disappear. It gets buried in the body, showing up as:

- Anxiety when love knocks again.
- Guilt for wanting to leave what no longer serves you.
- Shame for choosing happiness over duty.
- Resentment toward parents who never modeled healthy love.

Over time, **emotional baggage turns life upside down**. It clouds judgment, creates irrational fears, and manifests in physical symptoms- insomnia, chronic fatigue, heart palpitations, and unexplained tension in the body.

We carry invisible suitcases filled with regret, "what ifs," and emotional debts. And the more we carry, the harder it becomes to move freely, let alone love freely.

Choosing to Love Again: The Boldest Act of Self-Healing

To **love again after pain** is not betrayal to your past- it is **healing**. It is saying, "My story does not end in sadness." It is permitting yourself to evolve. The fear of remarriage or re-loving after a failed relationship is often rooted not in lack of love, but in the belief: "I don't deserve happiness," or "I will be hurt again." But emotional healing begins when we learn to **trust love again, not blind love, but conscious love.**

Conscious love respects boundaries. It values emotional freedom. It doesn't bind- it sets both people free to grow.

The Prison of Controlling Love

Many people mistake control for love. In dysfunctional relationships, love is used as currency: "If you love me, you'll do what I say." This conditional love creates deep emotional scars and makes one doubt their worth.

Control stems from fear: fear of abandonment, fear of losing power, fear of change. But **true love doesn't control; it liberates.** It encourages truth, even if it means parting ways.

To heal from this pattern, one must:

- Identify where love has become fear.
- Reclaim their voice from silence.
- Set boundaries with love, not resentment.
- Choose self-respect over societal validation.

Maya's Silent Struggle

Maya was married for 18 years. On the outside, it was a respectable, stable family. But inside, she was emotionally isolated. Her husband was not abusive, but he was emotionally unavailable, controlling, and dismissive. She lived like a ghost in her own home; her laughter forgotten, her dreams shelved.

She thought of leaving many times, but each time she imagined telling her children or her parents, guilt drowned her resolve. "What will people say?" became a louder voice than "What do I need?"

Eventually, after years of self-work, Maya left, not in rebellion, but in love. Love for herself. Love for the woman she once was and the woman she wanted to become.

Years later, she met someone who didn't complete her but **celebrated her completeness**. She realized that love isn't about filling a void, but about sharing your light with someone who respects it.

Letting Go Is Not Failure- It Is Freedom

We must understand that leaving a dysfunctional relationship or choosing love again after loss is not failure- it's an **act of courage**. We are not breaking the family; we are breaking the pattern.

You are not disloyal for choosing peace. You are not selfish for wanting to be emotionally whole. You are not weak for walking away- you are strong for listening to your soul's whisper over society's scream.

Conclusion: Break Free and Love Bravely

This chapter is a love letter to the soul that's been silent too long.

To the woman who stayed too long. To the man who gave up his dreams for duty. To the adult who still fears love because childhood taught them it hurts.

You deserve a love that heals, not haunts. You deserve a second chance at joy, not because the first didn't work, but because your heart is worthy of more.

Don't fear re-love. Don't fear endings. Love, in its purest form, always leads to truth. And truth-when embraced, sets us free.

Let's love again in the next chapter -fully, fiercely, and wisely.

Chapter 23:

Choosing Love Again - Healing Beyond the Wounds

Some hearts are not broken-they are just buried beneath layers of emotional dust, fear, and silence. In the tapestry of human relationships, the most painful knots are often formed in places where love was meant to blossom but instead was suffocated-within families, marriages, and broken bonds. This chapter is an invitation to confront the unspoken grief, the silent suffering, and the emotional paralysis that many endure while appearing strong on the outside.

The Silent Trauma of Dysfunctional Families

In many families, emotional wounds pass silently from generation to generation like heirlooms. Children raised in dysfunctional environments learn early to survive, not thrive. They absorb unspoken rules: *"Don't talk, don't feel, don't challenge."* Emotional needs are dismissed. Love is conditional. The truth is avoided.

These children grow up into adults who mistrust love, avoid vulnerability, and wear emotional armor. They often fear abandonment, but fear intimacy even more. They may stay in broken relationships simply because *"it's better than being alone,"*-repeating cycles that mirror their unresolved past.

"Trauma isn't always about what happened to you. Sometimes it's what should have happened but didn't."

The Fear of Divorce and Remarriage

In many cultures and families, divorce is not seen as a liberation but a failure. The stigma runs deep. People stay in emotionally damaging marriages for the sake of appearances, children, or social acceptance. Yet, beneath the surface, they are emotionally dying.

They fear what comes after- uncertainty, loneliness, judgment. But what they don't realize is that staying in a toxic or loveless relationship is also a form of emotional suicide. Choosing to walk away from something unhealthy is not a weakness. It's a radical act of self-respect.

And then there's the fear of loving again.

To open up again after heartbreak feels like standing at the edge of a cliff with no promise of a soft landing. But here's the truth: **love is never the problem- it's the absence of healing that causes the fear.** When we heal, we gain the wisdom to love with boundaries, self-awareness, and emotional clarity.

Emotional Baggage: The Hidden Saboteur

Unhealed emotions are like invisible anchors. You carry them everywhere, into new relationships, parenting, friendships, and even your relationship with yourself.

People often suppress their desires to love again, thinking they are being wise. But avoidance is not wisdom- it is fear disguised as maturity.

Suppressing love due to past pain does not protect you- it isolates you.

Emotional baggage is not your fault, but it is your responsibility to unpack it.

Every suppressed tear, every unspoken word, every betrayal never processed, creates internal pressure that eventually shows up as anxiety, illness, fatigue, or chronic dissatisfaction.

Raghav's Silent Battle-Choosing Love Beyond Pain

Raghav was a good husband and father who did everything in his power to give his family a comfortable, secure, and happy life. From financial stability to emotional presence, he fulfilled every role with quiet commitment. Yet, he lived in a home filled with criticism, blame, and emotional coldness.

His wife, Meera, constantly complained, never acknowledging his efforts. She often portrayed herself as the one doing everything for the family while accusing Raghav of doing nothing. In front of friends and relatives, she mocked and backbit him. At home, she constantly reminded him how he had failed as a husband, making him question his own worth.

What hurt the most wasn't the yelling or the complaints; it was the absence of connection. No shared laughter. No emotional intimacy. No gratitude. Just an icy silence and a growing distance that even their son began to sense.

At night, when the world slept, Raghav lay awake, wondering what went wrong. He had given everything. Why wasn't that enough? Raghav, despite the inner turmoil, kept saying to himself: *"I am not a good husband. I am giving my wife love, but maybe it's not enough."* He silenced his needs, suppressed his pain, and stayed in the marriage only for his son, out of fear of society, judgment, and guilt.

But the body always knows what the heart suppresses.

Raghav, though disciplined with his food, a regular at morning walks, and a non-smoker, began experiencing chronic fatigue. He started losing his appetite. Frequent body aches followed. Later, tests revealed elevated liver enzymes, and eventually, an autoimmune liver condition.

Doctors were surprised; "You're healthy. You've done everything right."

"Raghav, what emotion are you holding in your liver?"

But Raghav knew the truth. He was emotionally dying in a house where love had become a stranger.

He read about emotional toxicity and how unexpressed emotions poison the body, especially the liver, which stores resentment and suppressed rage.

Eventually, Raghav chose to **live again.** Not just exist for the sake of others.

He sat with his son and spoke the truth-gently, wisely, lovingly. He redefined his role as a father, not as someone who tolerates toxicity, but as someone who teaches strength through honesty.

He separated, not in anger, but in clarity. It was terrifying at first. But for the first time, he could breathe. His health improved, his eyes sparkled again, and his liver enzymes slowly returned to normal.

Years of this emotional stress, despite his healthy lifestyle, took a toll on his body-leading to liver problems and low immunity. Only when he began acknowledging his pain and choosing himself, again, did healing begin. He found his strength not in separation alone, but in emotional honesty, self-love, and the courage to live authentically.

And one day, in a quiet moment, Raghav looked in the mirror and whispered to himself,
"I chose love again.."

Insight

This story is not just about marriage or divorce. It's about the silent emotional suffering many men go through, being neglected, dismissed, and unacknowledged. It's about how love, when absent or distorted, can damage us not just emotionally but physically. It's about how self-love and emotional honesty can become the most courageous act of healing.

Whether you are a man or a woman, remember: choosing love again doesn't always mean choosing another person. It means choosing your peace. Choosing your well-being. Choosing to live, not just survive.

Healing Is a Choice- And It Begins Within

Healing begins the moment you stop blaming your past and start nurturing your present. You are not what happened to you. You are what you choose to become now. You don't have to wait for closure from another person. You can give yourself the peace and forgiveness that others failed to offer.

You can choose to:

- **Leave a toxic relationship** with grace.
- **Begin again,** even if your heart still trembles.
- **Fall in love** with yourself before you fall in love with someone else.
- **Speak your truth** even if your voice shakes.

Self-Therapies for Releasing Emotional Baggage

Let me offer you a few gentle self-therapies to begin your journey of emotional release and self-healing:

1. Letter Writing Ritual

Write a letter to the person or situation that caused you pain. Pour out every emotion. Don't censor yourself. When you're done, burn the letter or bury it-this is a symbolic act of letting go.

2. Mirror Work

Stand before a mirror. Look into your eyes and say:

- *"I see you."*
- *"I forgive you."*
- *"I love you."* Do this daily. You'll begin to feel a softening inside.

3. Body-Emotion Mapping

Sit quietly. Ask yourself: *Where do I feel my pain?* Is it in the chest? The throat? The stomach? Place your hand there. Breathe into it. Acknowledge the emotion and say, *"I release you with love."*

4. Affirmations for Emotional Freedom

Repeat:

- *"I am safe to feel."*
- *"It's okay to begin again."*
- *"I deserve love that doesn't hurt."*

5. Heart Meditation

Visualize your heart as a flower slowly opening with every breath. Inhale peace. Exhale fear. Let your heart remember what softness feels like.

A Story of ReLove: Meera's Second Spring

Meera stayed in her marriage for 18 years, convincing herself that endurance was strength. But inside, she was lonely. Her husband was emotionally unavailable and often cruel. When her daughter left for college, Meera chose herself for the first time.

She walked out-not to chase freedom, but to rediscover it.

At 47, she met a man who listened, who saw her. She felt the old fear rise: *"What if it ends like before?"* But this time, Meera had changed. She was no longer choosing from emptiness- she was choosing from fullness. She knew her worth.

Their love wasn't perfect, but it was honest. It was healing. It was proof that love after pain is possible- and often, more powerful.

Conclusion: You Can Choose Love Again

The greatest illusion is believing that emotional pain makes you unworthy of love. The truth is, your scars make you more capable of giving and receiving love. If you allow healing to flow.

Let go of the guilt. Release the fear. Learn to love without needing to lose yourself again.

Choosing love again is not about finding another person. It's about finding the courage to remain open, despite the pain. It's about saying:

"I've been hurt, but I'm still here. I still believe in love. And this time, I choose differently."

This is not weakness. This is a strength. This is alchemy.

In the final chapter, we will bring all the pieces together. The emotional alchemy, the healing, the power of love, and the beauty of becoming whole again-mind, body, and soul.

Chapter 24:

The Final Step - Emotions are Strength, Love is the Key & you are love

As we come to the final words of this journey, I want you to pause, take a deep breath, and feel your heartbeat. This is not just a rhythm- it is a reminder that you are alive, evolving, and full of untapped power. If you have come this far, you are already healing. You are already becoming. Let us reflect on the transformative journey we've undertaken. Through every chapter, we've delved into the profound connection between emotions, the mind, and the body. And now, as we draw the final curtain, I wish to leave you with one essential truth: emotions are your greatest strength, and love is the ultimate key to unlocking a life of health, healing, and happiness.

This chapter is not an ending- it is a new beginning. One where you no longer seek healing from the outside alone, but recognize that *you* are your greatest healer. Through the wisdom of love, the understanding of your emotions, and the courage to face your pain, you now hold the most powerful truth:

You are the key.

Love: The Eternal Healer

Love is not just an emotion; it is the lifeblood of our existence. It is the force that nurtures, connects, and transforms. Whether it's the gentle love of a parent, the passionate love of a partner, or the universal love we share with humanity, love has the power to rejuvenate both the mind and the body.

Science affirms what ancient wisdom has long proclaimed: love enhances longevity. Studies show that individuals who give and receive love experience lower stress levels, better heart health, and stronger immune systems. The hormones triggered by love, such as oxytocin, dopamine, and serotonin, create a cascade of positive effects, reducing inflammation, enhancing mental clarity, and promoting emotional resilience.

Rumi beautifully captures this in his timeless words:

"Love is the bridge between you and everything."

Emotions Are Messengers, Not Enemies

You've seen how emotions affect the body - how anger clings to the liver, how heartbreak strains the heart, how fear stiffens the spine. But these emotions are not curses. They are sacred messengers. They come bearing truth, unprocessed pain, and the blueprint for your growth.

Feel them. Listen to them. Permit them to speak. Because every suppressed tear, every unspoken word, and every quiet ache is simply love, asking to be felt.

Stress and the Absence of Love

In contrast, a life devoid of love or filled with unresolved emotional blocks can lead to stress, anxiety, and illness. Chronic stress floods the body with cortisol, a hormone that, when elevated for long periods, wreaks havoc on our physical and mental well-being. Stress narrows our vision, isolates us from others, and traps us in cycles of fear and defensiveness.

But love provides a way out. Love empowers us to approach life with openness rather than fear, with empathy rather than judgment. It teaches us to see beyond imperfections, to forgive, and to embrace the humanity in ourselves and others.

The Power of Inner Alchemy

Healing doesn't mean you forget the past. It means you alchemize it. You turn the darkness into light, the pain into purpose, the wound into wisdom. That is emotional alchemy. That is what this book has always been about.

True transformation doesn't come from denying pain- it comes from embracing it, learning from it, and choosing love *despite* it.

You have that power now.

The Ripple Effect of Love

True love-rooted in kindness, empathy, and understanding, creates ripples that extend far beyond the individual. It fosters deeper connections, enhances communication, and builds trust. Love inspires us to grow, to heal, and to become the best versions of ourselves. It teaches us to respond with grace in moments of tension, thus breaking the cycle of stress and promoting harmony.

When we prioritize love, we prioritize life. Love is the antidote to loneliness, the cure for resentment, and the spark that lights the path toward inner peace.

A Poem: Love's Embrace

In the quiet of the soul, love softly sings,

Binding hearts and mending wings.

Through joy and pain, it lights the way,

A beacon bright, night or day.

Let love's truth seep into your core,

Unlock its magic, and open the door.

For love is the healer, the power, the key,

To live a life of vitality, wild and free.

Love and Longevity

The relationship between love and longevity cannot be overstated. People in loving relationships, whether with a partner, family, or community, are more likely to live longer, healthier lives. Love reduces the risk of cardiovascular diseases, improves mental health, and fosters an overall sense of well-being.

But love isn't limited to grand romantic gestures. Small acts of kindness, a simple hug, or words of appreciation can flood the brain with happiness hormones. These seemingly trivial moments accumulate to create a reservoir of joy and vitality.

Emotional Expression: The Gateway to Freedom

True love also thrives on honest emotional expression. Suppressing emotions can lead to a buildup of stress, resentment, and unresolved pain that manifests physically. Couples who share minimal communication or avoid conflict for the sake of appearances often experience health challenges, such as liver dysfunction or chronic fatigue. The body keeps score of our unspoken emotions, and the price is often paid in physical ailments.

Conversely, expressing emotions, be it through words, art, or acts of love, frees us from the chains of emotional suppression. It allows us to heal and connect deeply with ourselves and others.

Daily Self-Therapies for Emotional Healing

As promised, here are some tools to support your emotional health long after this book is closed. These practices can be woven into your daily life, gently bringing healing and strength from within.

1. The Mirror Talk (Self-Love Practice)
Stand in front of the mirror, look into your own eyes, and say:
"I am proud of you. I love you. I'm here for you. I forgive you."
Do this every day. Watch how your relationship with yourself transforms.

2. Emotional Journaling
Each evening, write freely for 10 minutes. Let your pen speak the truth of your heart. Don't edit. Don't censor. Just release.
Let your journal become your sanctuary.

3. Guided Breath & Heart Coherence

Close your eyes. Inhale deeply for 4 counts, hold for 4, exhale for 6. Focus on your heart. Imagine it glowing with light. Breathe love into it. Do this for 5-10 minutes daily to balance the heart and nervous system.

4. Emotional Art Expression

Paint, draw, sculpt, dance. Let your body express what words cannot. Artistic expression helps release blocked emotions and turns pain into beauty.

5. The Forgiveness Letter

Write a letter to someone who hurt you (or to yourself). Say everything you've been holding in. You don't have to send it. Just let it go. Then burn or tear it with intention, releasing the burden from your body.

6. The Inner Child Dialogue

Close your eyes. Imagine your younger self sitting beside you. Ask them:
"What do you need from me?"
Listen, respond, and offer the love they never received. Reparent yourself with gentleness.

7. Body-Emotion Mapping Meditation

Lie down. Scan your body. Where do you feel tightness, pain, or heaviness? Place your hand there. Ask, "What emotion are you holding?"
Listen. Breathe love into that space. Let it soften.

You Are Not Broken

You are not too much.
You are not weak for feeling deeply.
You are not broken; you are *becoming*.

In a world that taught you to silence your heart, you are learning to listen. That is divine. That is brave. That is love.

A Final Thought: Embrace the Strength of Love

As you close this book, remember that love is not a luxury; it is a necessity. Love empowers us to rise above our challenges, to find meaning in our struggles, and to create a life of happiness and health. It is the foundation of emotional well-being, the cornerstone of physical health, and the guiding force toward a fulfilled and purposeful life.

Every emotion you feel is an opportunity to grow, to heal, and to love. Accept these emotions with grace, process them with understanding, and let love be your guide. When you do, you will unlock the door to a life of extraordinary health, happiness, and harmony.

Conclusion: The Journey Continues

This book has been a guide to understanding the transformative power of emotions and their direct connection to your body and mind. By embracing emotional health, you've taken the first step toward a life of happiness, well-being, and self-discovery.

Remember, emotions are not your enemies. They are your greatest teachers. And love is the key that unlocks the doors to emotional freedom, happiness, and healing. Embrace love, live authentically, and trust that your journey toward emotional health will lead to a vibrant and fulfilled life

This book has been a guide to understanding the intricate dance between emotions, love, and well-being. It is not the end but the beginning of your emotional journey. As you move forward, may you embrace every emotion with courage, every relationship with love, and every moment with gratitude. Remember: emotions are your strength, and love is your key.

Final Words: A Love Letter to the Reader

If this book has touched even a small part of your heart, know that it is your own heart calling you home.

May you never again shrink to fit someone's comfort.
May you rise, rooted in your truth.
May you always choose love, not just for others, but for yourself.

Let your emotions be your compass.
Let your love be your legacy.

You are not alone.
You are seen.
You are worthy.
You are free.

With all my heart,
I thank you.
For reading, for feeling, for healing.
The journey continues in you.

Self-Healing Toolkit: Reclaiming Your Emotional Power

1. Journaling Prompts: Conversations with Your Inner Self

Writing is therapy. Use these prompts to connect deeply with your emotions:

- What emotion am I feeling right now, and where do I feel it in my body?
- What is this emotion trying to tell me?
- What do I need to forgive myself for today?
- What do I need to forgive someone else for?
- What would my inner child want me to know right now?
- What does self-love look like for me today?

---

2. Breathwork & Grounding Practices

Your breath is your bridge between your body and soul.

3-Minute Grounding Exercise

- Sit comfortably and place your hand on your heart.
- Breathe in for 4 seconds, hold for 4, exhale for 6.
- Repeat for 3 minutes, saying silently:

"I am safe. I am loved. I am home within myself."

Nature Grounding Ritual

- Walk barefoot on grass or soil.
- Visualize roots growing from your feet into the Earth.
- Say aloud: *"I release what no longer serves me."*

---

3. Mirror Work: Love in Your Eyes

Healing begins when you start seeing yourself with compassion.

- Stand in front of a mirror.
- Look into your eyes and say:

"I love you. I see your pain. I honor your strength."

- Repeat this daily for 7 days and feel the shift.

4. Affirmations by Body Part & Emotion

Emotion	Body Part Affected	Healing Affirmation
Sadness	Lungs	"I release grief and breathe in love."
Anger	Liver	"I am free from anger. I welcome peace."
Fear	Kidneys	"I am safe and protected in all that I do."
Heartbreak	Heart	"I am open to love. My heart is whole."
Shame	Stomach	"I honor myself. I am enough just as I am."

5. Emotional Release Techniques

Tear Therapy

Permit yourself to cry. Crying is a sacred act of release; it clears the energy body and brings emotional clarity.

The Pillow Scream

When overwhelmed with frustration or suppressed anger:

- Scream into a pillow.
- Punch or press it firmly.
- Journal afterward to reflect on the release.

Sound Healing Playlist

Create a playlist of songs that mirror your current emotion. Let the music move through you. Dance, sway, or simply breathe with it.

---

6. Heart-Healing Ritual

A gentle practice to reconnect with love.

- Light a candle. Sit with a photo of someone you love, or yourself.
- Place your hands on your heart.
- Say: *"I give myself the love I've been seeking. I deserve love. I am in love."*
- Send silent blessings to yourself and anyone you feel called to forgive or reconnect with.

---

7. Release Under the Moon (Monthly Ritual)

Every full moon:

- Write down what emotions, memories, or beliefs you wish to release.

- Read them aloud and burn the paper (safely).
- Say: *"I let go. I rise. I am free."*

---

8. Emergency Emotional SOS Kit

When you're triggered or overwhelmed:

- Pause & Breathe: Inhale for 4, hold for 4, exhale for 6.
- Ground Yourself: Place your feet on the floor. Feel your body.
- Hydrate: Drink a glass of water.
- Write: "What am I feeling right now? Why?"
- Hug Yourself. Literally.

Closing Whisper:

You were never broken; only buried under layers of pain, conditioning, and unspoken emotions. This toolkit is your sacred key to return home to yourself.

You are worthy of healing.
You are worthy of love.
And your healing helps heal the world.

The path to a vibrant and fulfilled life is now in your hands. Let love lead the way.

References (APA Style)

Online Sources

American Psychological Association. (n.d.). *Monitor on Psychology.* https://www.apa.org/monitor

Greater Good Science Center. (n.d.). *Science-based insights for a meaningful life.* University of California, Berkeley. https://greatergood.berkeley.edu

Harvard Health Publishing. (n.d.). *Positive psychology: Harnessing the power of happiness, mindfulness, and inner strength.* https://www.health.harvard.edu

National Institute of Mental Health. (n.d.). *Emotions and mental health.* https://www.nimh.nih.gov/health/topics/emotions

Google wikipedias

www.ingramcontent.com/pod-product-compliance
Lightning Source LLC
Chambersburg PA
CBHW062149150726
47991CB00006B/2218